The Enemy on the Tide

THE WEST VIEW OF DOVER-CASTLE, IN THE COUNTY OF KENT.

DOVER CASTLE, KENT

The Enemy on the Tide

The Coastal Defences of England from the Roman Period to the 19th Century

English Coast Defences
George Clinch

The Battle of the Channel Tunnel and
Dover Castle and Forts
by Thomas Berney

LEONAUR

The Enemy on the Tide
The Coastal Defences of England from the Roman Period to the 19th Century
by George Clinch
The Battle of the Channel Tunnel and Dover Castle and Forts
by Thomas Berney

FIRST EDITION

First published under the titles
English Coast Defences
and
The Battle of the Channel Tunnel and Dover Castle and Forts

Leonaur is an imprint of Oakpast Ltd

ISBN: 978-1-78282-375-9 (hardcover)
ISBN: 978-1-78282-376-6 (softcover)

http://www.leonaur.com

Publisher's Notes

Contents

To
THE RIGHT HONOURABLE
ARTHUR JAMES BALFOUR, M.P.
FIRST LORD OF THE ADMIRALTY
THESE PAGES ARE
INSCRIBED

Preface

The intricate coast-line of England, so difficult for an enemy to blockade, so difficult at every point for combined naval and military forces to defend against raiders, presents to the student of history an extremely interesting subject. It is to its insularity that England owes something of its greatness, and to the great length of its coast-line that its vulnerability is due.

The present book represents the results of a study of the methods and means by which England, from Roman times down to the early years of the nineteenth century, has defended her shores against various over-sea enemies, who have attempted, sometimes successfully, to invade and conquer.

Part 1

Roman Occupation

Prehistoric Camps

Round the coast of England there are many prehistoric earthworks of great extent and strength. These fall generally under the heads of hill-top fortresses and promontory camps. The works comprised under the former head are so arranged as to take the greatest possible advantage of natural hill-tops, often of large size. On the line where the comparatively level top developed into a more or less precipitous slope a deep ditch was dug, and the earth so removed was in most cases thrown outwards so as to form a rampart which increased the original difficulties of the sloping hillside.

The latter type of earthwork, called promontory camps from their natural conformation, were strengthened by the digging of a deep ditch, so as to cut off the promontory from the main table-land from which it projected, and in some cases the sides of the camp were made more precipitous by artificial scarping.

An examination of these types of earthworks leads to the conclusion that they were probably tribal enclosures for the safe-guarding of cattle, etc.; that, strictly speaking, they were not military works at all, and, in any case, had no relation to national defence against enemies coming over-sea.

One finds in different parts of the country a prevalent tradition that the Romans occupied the more ancient British hill-top strongholds, and the name "Caesar's Camp" is popularly applied to many of them. If such an occupation really took place it was, in all probability, only of a temporary character. These fortifications were not suitable to the Roman method of military operations and encampment, and such archaeological evidences of Roman occupation as have been found point to the presence of domestic buildings, such as at Chanctonbury

Ring and Wolstanbury Camp (Sussex) rather than military works.

However, the question must not be dismissed as entirely without some foundation in fact, because it was only natural that the Roman invaders who dispossessed the Britons of their fastnesses should themselves have taken temporary possession of the works from which the Britons were driven out.

The Roman Invasion of Britain

There is hardly a single detail of the first invasion of Britain by the Romans which has not been the subject of dispute or discussion among historians and antiquaries, but, briefly, it may be stated as highly probable that Caesar left Portus Itius (Boulogne) on 25 August 55 B.C., and landed at or near what is now Deal on the following day.

When Caesar found a convenient time for the invasion of Britain, he got together about eighty transports, which he considered would be sufficient for carrying two legions across the channel. Those galleys which he had left he distributed to the *questor*, lieutenants, and officers of the cavalry. In addition to these ships there were eighteen transports, detained by contrary winds at a port about eight miles off, and these were appointed to carry over the cavalry.

A favourable breeze sprang up, and anchor was weighed about one in the morning. The cavalry in the eighteen other transports embarked at the other port. It was ten o'clock when Caesar reached the coast of Britain, where he saw the cliffs covered with the enemy's forces. He speaks of the place as being bounded by steep mountains in a way which clearly describes Dover and the eminences in its neighbourhood, comprising Shakespeare's Cliff, the western and eastern heights, and all the magnificent cliff of precipitous chalk rock which extends to Kingsdown, near Walmer. On such a coast as this, apart from the presence of the enemy, landing was impossible, and Caesar wisely determined to sail eight miles further on, where he found, probably at Deal, a plain and open shore. Caesar's description is most interesting, and may be quoted:

But the barbarians perceiving our design, sent their cavalry and chariots before, which they frequently make use of in battle, and following with the rest of their forces, endeavoured to oppose our landing: and indeed we found the difficulty very great on many accounts; for our ships being large, required a great depth of water; and the soldiers, who were wholly unacquainted with the places, and had their hands embarrassed and loaden with a weight of armour, were at the same time to leap from the ships, stand breast high against the waves, and encounter the enemy, while they, fighting upon dry ground, or advancing only a little way into the water, having the free use of all their limbs, and in places which they perfectly knew, could boldly cast their darts, and spur on their horses, well inured to that kind of service. All these circumstances serving to spread a terror among our men, who were wholly strangers to this way of fighting, they pushed not the enemy with the same vigour and spirit as was usual for them in combats upon dry ground.

Caesar, observing this, ordered some galleys, a kind of shipping less common with the barbarians, and more easily governed and put in motion, to advance a little from the transports towards the shore, in order to set upon the enemy in flank, and by means of their engines, slings, and arrows, drive them to some distance. This proved of considerable service to our men, for what with the surprise occasioned by the make of our galleys, the motion of the oars, and the playing of the engines, the enemy were forced to halt, and in a little time began to give back.

But our men still demurring to leap into the sea, chiefly because of the depth of the water in those parts, the standard-bearer of the tenth legion, having first invoked the gods for success, cried out aloud: 'Follow me, fellow-soldiers, unless you will betray the Roman eagle into the hands of the enemy; for my part, I am resolved to discharge my duty to Caesar and the common-wealth.' Upon this he jumped into the sea, and advanced with the eagle against the enemy: whereat, our men exhorted one another to prevent so signal a disgrace, all that were in the ship followed him, which being perceived by those in the nearest vessels, they also did the like, and boldly approached the enemy.

The battle was obstinate on both sides; but our men, as being neither able to keep their ranks, nor get firm footing, nor follow their respective standards, because leaping promiscuously from their ships, every one joined the first ensign he met, were thereby thrown into great confusion. The enemy, on the other hand, being well acquainted with the shallows, when they saw our men advancing singly from the ships, spurred on their horses, and attacked them in that perplexity.

In one place great numbers would gather round a handful of Romans; others falling upon them in flank, galled them mightily with their darts, which Caesar observing, ordered some small boats to be manned, and ply about with recruits. By this means the foremost ranks of our men having got footing, were followed by all the rest, when falling upon the enemy briskly, they were soon put to the rout. But as the cavalry were not yet arrived, we could not pursue or advance far into the island, which was the only thing wanting to render the victory complete.[1]

Sea-fighting was not unknown to the Romans, but as far as the invasion of Britain was concerned, Caesar's fleet may be regarded as a collection of ships for transport purposes rather than a fighting naval force. The main object of Caesar was to land his soldiers so that they might encounter and vanquish the enemy on dry land. This, as the graphic words of the *Commentaries* clearly tell, was quickly accomplished. The British method of fighting, in which chariots were employed for the attack, is described by Caesar,[2] who was evidently impressed by their skilful combination of rapid and awe-inspiring attack with the freedom and mobility of light infantry.

It is noteworthy that Caesar says nothing about coast defences in the form of earthworks, or indeed in any other form, and it is on other grounds improbable that the Britons possessed any provision of that kind against invading enemies, although they themselves lived in stockaded enclosures.

The Romans were the first people to introduce anything like general coast defence in Britain, and in this, as in all other branches of their military enterprises, they displayed great skill, intelligence, and thoroughness. For the defence of the coast of the eastern and southern parts of Britain they erected a chain of *castra* or fortresses extending

---

1. *Commentaries on the Gallic War.* 2. "Their way of fighting-with their chariots is this: first they drive their chariots on all sides, and throw their darts, insomuch that by the very terror of the horses, and noise of the wheels, they often break the ranks of the enemy. When they have forced their way into the midst of the cavalry, they quit their chariots and fight on foot: meanwhile the drivers retire a little from the combat, and place themselves in such a manner as to favour the retreat of their countrymen, should they be overpowered by the enemy. Thus in action they perform the part both of nimble horsemen and stable infantry; and by continual exercise and use have arrived at that expertness, that in the most steep and difficult places they can stop their horses upon a full stretch, turn them which way they please, run along the pole, rest on the harness, and throw themselves back into their chariots with incredible dexterity." (*Comm. on the Gallic War*, iv, xxix).

from Brancaster, on the north-west coast of Norfolk, to Porchester, situated on the extreme north-west shore of Portsmouth Harbour.

The position of the various fortresses shows that it was not necessary, according to the Roman plan of defence, that one fort should command views of its neighbours. Reculver and Richborough, Richborough and Dover, Dover and Lymne, Lymne and Pevensey, were in no case visible from each other, although the distance which separated them was not great in every case. Under these circumstances it is not remarkable to find evidences, as will presently be explained, of special provision for signalling between the fortresses.

THE COUNT OF THE SAXON SHORE

During the early part of the Roman occupation of Britain the chief mode of defence adopted against piratical incursions was the navy, *classis Britannica*. This, for the most part, moved in those waters which lay between the British and Gaulish coasts, answering to what we now know as the Straits of Dover and the southern part of the North Sea.

For a time the navy was able to keep the seas free from pirates, but towards the end of the third century the trouble became greater than ever. Raiders came in large numbers both to our own coasts and also to the Continental coasts opposite, to both of which the name of the Saxon Shore was given. The Romans decided to take strong measures to put an end to the trouble. For this purpose they appointed a special officer, one Marcus Aurelius Valerius Carausius, commonly known by his last name.

The appearance of Carausius on the stage of history brings into prominence a man of strong but unscrupulous character. He is believed to have allowed the pirates to carry on their work of plunder at their pleasure, and then, having waited for the proper moment, he relieved them of their booty on the return journey. In this way he acquired great riches, and in due course he employed the fleet, not against the enemy of Rome, but against Rome, and in such a way as to render Britain independent. After several ineffectual attempts to break his power, Diocletian and Maximianus found it necessary to recognize him as their colleague in the empire, a triumph which Carausius commemorated by striking a medal bearing as a device three busts with appropriate emblems the legend:

(*ob.*) *CARAVSIVS. ET. FRATRES. SVI*
(*rev.*)   *PAX AVGGG.*

Carausius was murdered by his chief official, Allectus, in the year 293. Shortly after his death, and when the British province had ceased to be independent of Rome, an official was appointed called the Count of the Saxon Shore.

This officer, whose title was *Comes Littoris Saxonici,* was a high official whose duty it was to command the defensive forces and supervise the fortresses erected on the east, south-east, and south coasts of England against the piratical raids of the various tribes of Saxons and others during the latter part of the Roman occupation of Britain. The precise nature of his duties and the full extent of his authority are equally unknown, but they probably comprised the general oversight and command both of the fortresses on the British coast from the northern coast of Norfolk to a point near Portsmouth, and the navy which guarded our shores.

Opinions are divided on the question as to what was precisely meant by the phrase "*the Saxon shore.*" Was it, as some think, those parts of the shore of Britain and Gaul on which, being specially subject to Saxon raiders, defences were erected or employed for repelling the invaders? Or was it, as others have supposed, perhaps with less probability, a strip of territory following the line of coast nearest the sea on which the Saxons were allowed to settle in late Roman times?

Roman Coast Fortresses

A careful examination of the fortresses which protected the line of coast to which reference has been made, is likely, we think, to afford some light upon the above-mentioned point. If we pay attention to the plans of these fortresses, it will be obvious that at least two, Reculver and Brancaster, belong to a type of Roman fortress which is associated with a period much earlier than the time, as far as we know, when Saxon or other raiders began to molest the coasts of Britain and Gaul. Perhaps it is significant that these two *castra* command the entrance to two of the great water ways on our east coast, the Thames and the Wash. The other seven fortresses, judging from their plans, belong to a later stage of development in Roman military architecture.

From this and other features already described we may infer that the whole series of fortresses was built at different periods, and probably in the following order:

Reculver.	Richborough.
Brancaster.	Lymne.
Porchester.	Pevensey.

Unfortunately, the architectural remains of the remaining *castra* are not sufficiently perfect to allow of classification.

One or two of the coast fortresses, such as Pevensey and Lymne, may well have been erected towards the close of the Roman occupation. It is significant that tiles bearing the impressed name of Honorius have been found built into the walls of Pevensey, pointing to the lateness of the building of at least some of the masonry at that *castrum*.[3]

At Lymne early inscriptions, etc. have been found built into the walls, indicating a period if not late in the Roman period, at least a considerable time after the date of the inscribed stones which were enclosed, as mere building material, in the walls. This is corroborated by indications of adhering barnacles, from which we may fairly conclude that there was a period of submergence between the time of the carving and the subsequent use as building material.

It seems probable, therefore, that although the earlier fortresses may have been intended to serve as centres for the Roman army, they may have been supplemented at a later period by other *castra*, forming altogether a chain of defences intended to protect the shores of Britain against Saxon invaders.

The late Mr. G. E. Fox, F.S.A., who made a special study of the subject, writes as follows:[4]

By the last quarter of the third century the Romano-British fleet, on which no doubt dependence had been placed for the protection of the east and south coasts from raids by plundering bands of rovers from over the seas, had evidently failed to afford that protection. Whether it was that the fleet was not numerous enough, or for whatever reason, the Roman government determined to supplement its first line of defence by a second, and this was achieved by the erection of forts capable of holding from 500 to 1,000 men each, on points of the coast-line extending from the mouth of the Wash to Pevensey on the coast of Sussex. The coast-line indicated received the name of *Litus Saxonicum*, and the nine fortresses which guarded it are called 'the forts of the Saxon Shore.'

The following were the nine fortresses referred to with the modern place-names:

---

3. See page 41.
4. *Victoria History of Suffolk*, i, 282.

1. Branodunum.	Brancaster.
2. Gariannonum.	Burgh Castle (near Yarmouth).
3. Othona.	Bradwell-on-Sea.
4. Regulbium.	Reculver.
5. Rutupiae.	Richborough.
6. Dubris.	Dover.
7. Portus Lemanus.	Lymne.
8. Anderida.	Pevensey.
9. Portus Magnus.	? Porchester.

It will be observed that the various fortresses in this chain of defensive works occur at irregular distances on or near the coast-line, and on examination it will be found that in most cases good reason exists for the selection of the various sites.

1. BRANODUNUM

There is sufficient evidence to identify the Roman fort of Branodunum with some ruins lying to the east of Brancaster, a village situated near the north-western corner of Norfolk, on the shores of the Wash. The only early mention of the place is found in the *Notitia Imperii*, a catalogue of the distribution of the imperial military, naval, and civilian officers throughout the Roman world. From this remarkable work, a compilation which has come down to us from a very early period, it appears that the *Comes Littoris Saxonici* (the Count of the Saxon Shore) had under him nine subordinate officers, called *praepositi*, distributed round the coasts of Norfolk, Essex, Kent, Sussex, and Hampshire. The fortress at Brancaster is now in a very much ruined state, and but little can be gathered of its original form from a casual or superficial examination. Excavations and careful searches made about the middle of the nineteenth century brought to light many facts about its plan.[5] The fortress was a square of 190 yards and the angles were irregularly rounded. Exclusive of *ashlar*, the walls were found to be 10 feet thick, and bounded with large blocks of white sandstone. At one of the roughly rounded angles the *ashlar* facing remained intact. It consisted of blocks of sandstone firmly set in mortar with joints of three inches minimum thickness.

Traces were found within the walls of small apartments adjoining the main walls into which the smaller walls were regularly bonded, pointing to contemporaneity of the work.

---

5. Archaeological Institute, Norwich volume, 1851, pp. 9–16.

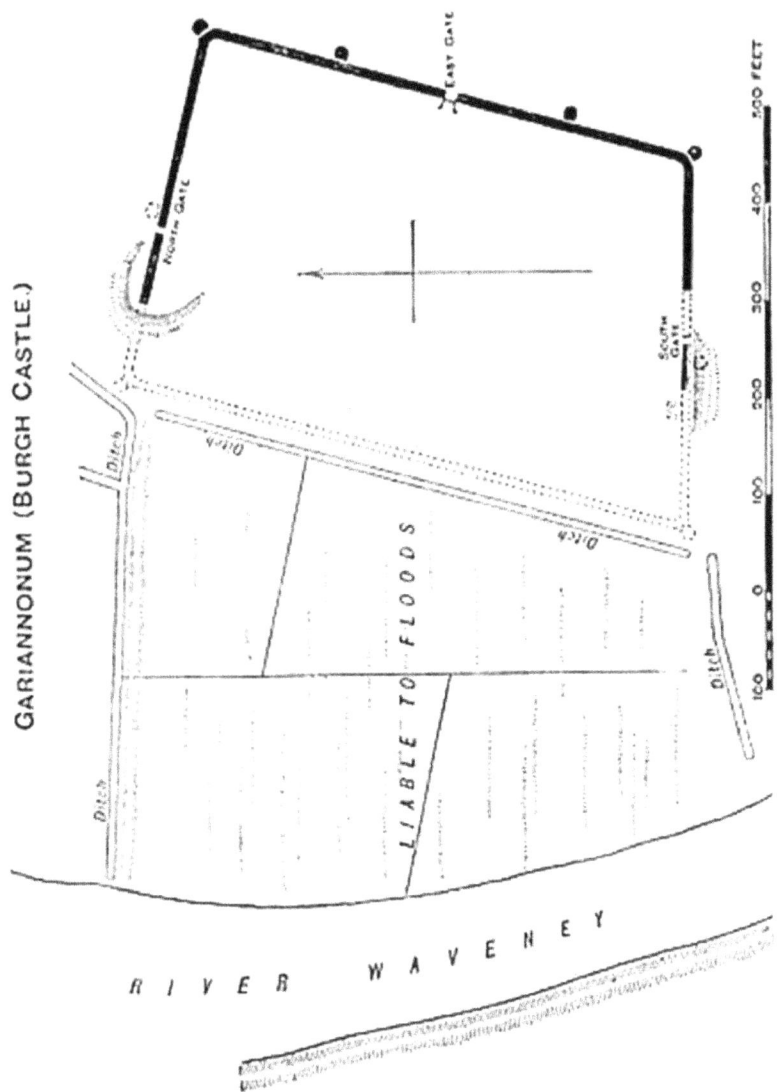

GARIANNONUM (BURGH CASTLE.)

NORTH GATE

EAST GATE

SOUTH GATE

RIVER WAVENEY

LIABLE TO FLOODS

Ditch

Ditch

Ditch

Ditch

Ditch

500 FEET
400
300
200
100
0
100

FIG. 1

Two facts of some importance are proved by the excavations, *viz.* (1) the strength of the fortress as a defensive work, and (2) the simple and early character of the plan. Traces of gates were observed in the eastern and western walls.

2. GARIANNONUM

Now known as Burgh Castle, is situated in Suffolk near the point where the Rivers Yare and Waveney fall into Breydon Water. The lines of its walls enclose a space, roughly speaking, 660 feet by 330 feet, over four acres. It is generally considered to be one of the most perfect Roman buildings remaining in the kingdom. The walls in places remain to a height of 9 feet, and their foundations are no less than 12 feet in thickness. The bastions, or perhaps more correctly, towers, which flank the gates and support the rounded angles of the walls are of peculiar, pear-shaped plan. They are solid, and to the height of about 7 feet are not tied into the walls. Above that height, however, they are bonded into the walls with which, curious as it may appear, they are undoubtedly coeval. It is noteworthy that there are two bastions on the east side and one each on the north and south sides, and that they, six in all, are provided with a hole in the top, 2 feet wide and 2 feet deep, indicating in all probability that they once mounted turntables upon which *ballistae* were placed for the defence of the fortress.

The masonry is of the kind which is usually found in Roman buildings, namely, a rubble core with courses of bonding tiles, and an outer facing of flints chipped to a flat surface.

Gariannonum was a place of great importance in Roman times. Here was stationed the captain of the Stablesian horse, styled Gariannonensis, under the command of *Comes littoris Saxonici.*

Walton.—Near Felixstowe, situated on what is now the foreshore, but which originally was a cliff 100 feet high, and commanding extensive views of the surrounding country, are the ruins of what was an important Roman station. Although possibly not ranking as one of the nine great coast fortresses, it occupied a most important site for the defence of this part of the east coast of Britain, and commanded not only the entrance to the River Deben, but also all the adjacent coast to the south of it. Almost every trace of the station has now been obliterated by the waves, but from plans which have been preserved it appears that its plan was that of an oblong with towers or bastions at each angle. [6]

6. *Victoria History of Suffolk*, i, 278.

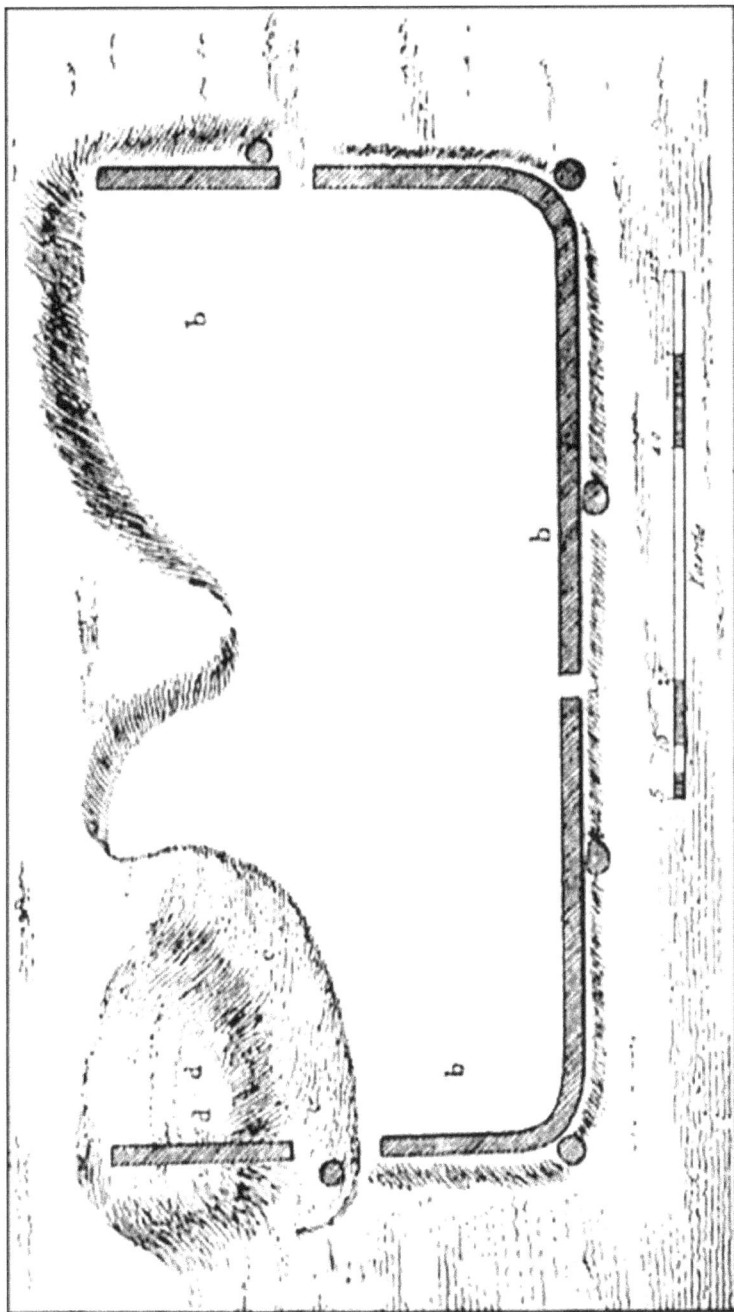

Fig. 2. Plan of Roman Walls, Etc., at Gariannonum (Burgh Castle 1776)

3. OTHONA

Or Ithanchester, near Bradwell-on-Sea, in Essex, was another important member of the Roman coast defences of Britain. It commanded the entrances of the Rivers Blackwater and Colne. Little now remains of Othona, although it is on record that the fortress enclosed an area of 4 acres, and that its walls possessed foundations no less than 14 feet in thickness.

The defence of such a point as this against the incursions of foes was a matter of much importance, because this was a point on the coast of Britain specially susceptible to attack by marauders, and, as we shall see, special precautions were taken against attacks of this kind.

At a distance of about four miles to the north of Othona, across the estuary of the River Blackwater, lies the island of Mersea. In the year 1896 some Roman foundations were accidentally discovered in the western part of the island which, upon examination, appear to have an important bearing on the Roman scheme of coast defence in this part of Britain. The foundations were circular, 65 feet in diameter, and closely resembling in gigantic form the steering-wheel of a ship.

The foundations were of Kentish rag and chalk lime mortar, and above this the low walling was almost entirely composed of Roman bricks set in red mortar. Dr. Henry Laver, F.S.A., who communicated the discovery to the Society of Antiquaries of London,[7] modestly abstains from giving any explanation or theory as to the purpose of the building which stood on this site, but in the opinion of the present writer there seems to be little doubt that the foundations were intended to carry a lofty *pharos*, or perhaps signalling tower of timber by means of which messages might have been transmitted to Othona and Colchester.

4. REGULBIUM

Now known as Reculver, is situated about three miles to the east of Herne Bay. The site, although originally some distance inland, is now, owing to the encroachment of the sea, quite close to the shore. Indeed, about half of its area has been destroyed by the waves, and is now covered at high water. Its area when complete was over seven acres, and its walls which, in the eighteenth century, stood 10 feet high, and still remain to a height of 8 feet in some places, are no less than 8 feet in thickness with two sets-off inside. It seems doubtful whether there

---

7. Proceedings, xvi, 422-429.

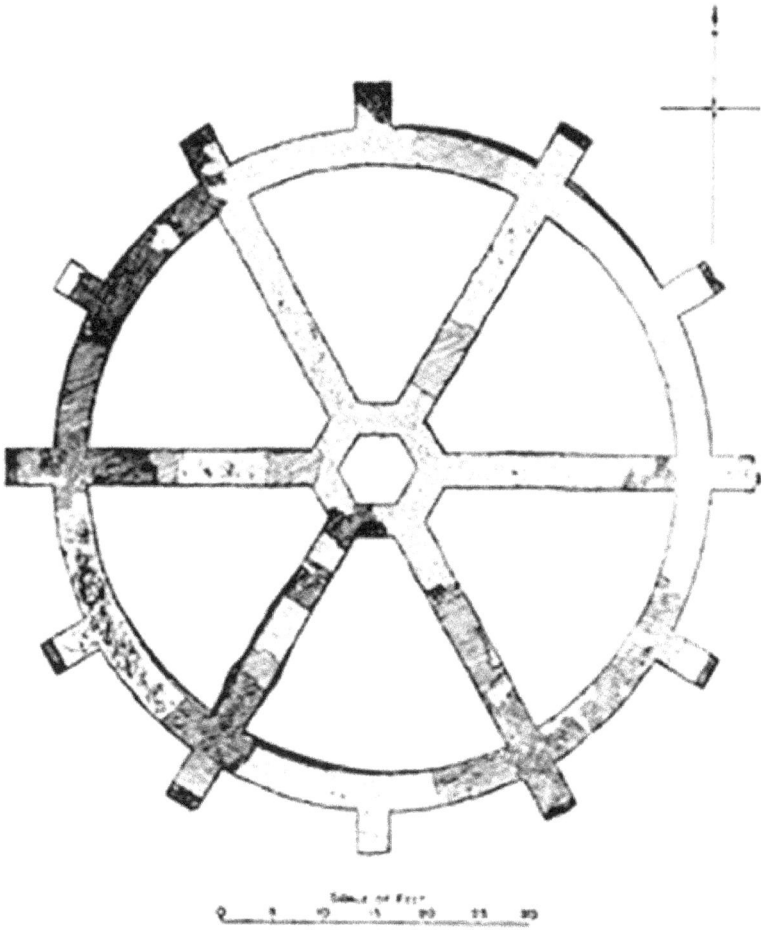

FIG. 3. PLAN OF ROMAN BUILDING, WEST MERSEA, ESSEX

REGULBIUM (RECULVER)

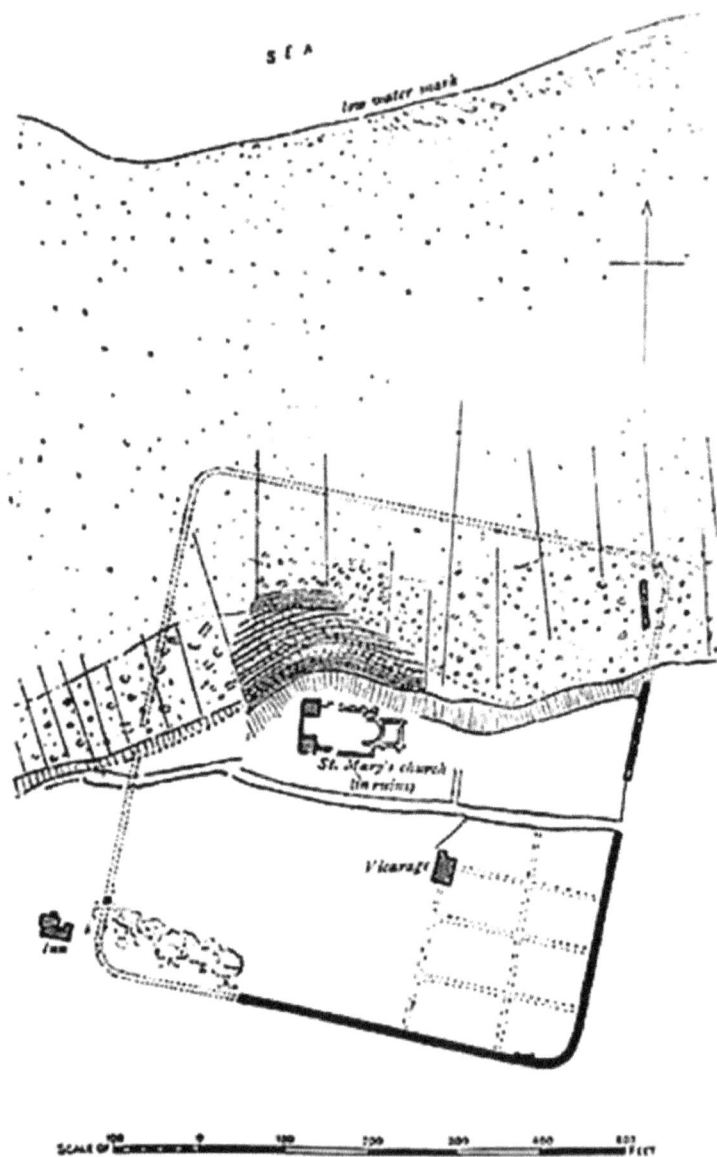

FIG. 4. RECULVER, KENT

was ever a ditch round the castrum. Owing to the ruinous condition of the main part of the masonry, and the complete destruction which has overtaken the northern part of the foundations, it is impossible to ascertain any particulars as to the gates or internal arrangements.

As will be seen from the accompanying ground-plan the form of the *castrum* at Reculver was quadrangular. The angles were rounded, but there are no indications of towers or bastions. These features are considered characteristic of Roman fortresses of early date. Another feature pointing to the same conclusion is the absence of tile courses in the walls.

The only recorded facts about this fortress is a mention in the *Notitia*, from which we learn that it was garrisoned by the first *cohort* of the Vetasians commanded by a *tribune*.

At a comparatively early stage in the art of Roman masonry in Britain the idea was conceived of protecting the enclosing wall of the fortress by means of projecting bastions and towers. In an early type represented in the Romano-British coast fortresses, of which this of Reculver is an excellent illustration, there were, as we have seen, no projections whether of walls, bastions, towers, or gates. Reliance was placed in the strength and solidity of the walls themselves, which were 8 feet in thickness. But the desirability of having some points from which the enemy could be attacked in flank whilst battering the wall soon became evident, and in other cases such as Richborough, Lymne, Pevensey, etc., we find that the fortress was furnished not only with massive walls, but also with strong angle-towers and bastions or towers at intervals by which the wall could be commanded and protected.

These various works furnish an interesting series of illustrations of the progress made in the military architecture of the period.

5. Rutupiae

Now known as Richborough, situated about two miles north-north-west of Sandwich, was a station of great importance in the Roman period, being then, as Sandwich was subsequently for many years, the chief British port for travellers and traffic to and from the Continent. In shape Rutupiae was a rectangular parallelogram, with the greater length from east to west. Its walls, which were lofty and massive, enclosed an area of somewhat less than 6 acres. At each angle is, or was, a circular bastion 18 feet 6 inches in diameter, and square towers or bastions at intervals projected beyond the general face of the walls.

FIG. 5. ROMAN MASONRY, RECULVER, KENT SHOWING FACING STONES (SQUARED), RUBBLE CORE, AND PEBBLY FOUNDATIONS

Fig. 6. Reculver: The Ruins of the Church

A considerable part of the south-east corner, and the whole of the east wall have been destroyed by the falling of the cliff in the direction of the River Stour. The theory formerly propounded that the *castrum* had no eastern wall has been disproved by the careful examinations of Mr. G. E. Fox and other eminent antiquaries. These examinations have definitely shown that large fragments of the east wall have fallen down the cliff. It is certain that the *castrum* of Rutupiae as also those of Regulbium and Portus Lemanis, in spite of the doubt which has been expressed in each instance, had four walls.

The chief peculiarity of Rutupiae is the presence of a solid mass of masonry underground, a little to the east rather than in the middle of the enclosed space. Many different theories have been put forward to account for its purpose, but it is now generally agreed that it was intended to serve as the foundation for a lofty structure, perhaps of timber, the purpose of which was for signalling between this station and that at Reculver, and possibly also answering to the *pharos* at Dover. It is not improbable that it also served as a lighthouse for ships entering the estuary of the Stour from the sea. If lights or signals could be seen as far as Dover they might from that point be communicated easily to and fro from the coast of France from the high ground on which the *pharos* of Dover stands.

In order to understand the functions and relative positions of Regulbium and Rutupiae as coast fortresses during the Roman period, it is necessary to reconstruct the ancient geography of the north-eastern part of Kent. The small stream now falling into the sea near Reculver was at the period under consideration a river sufficiently broad and deep to afford a convenient channel for shipping. It was known as the Wantsum. Boats and ships voyaging from the French coast as well as from the British coast near Dover to London, usually took their course through the channel formed by the Stour and the Wantsum, thus avoiding the strong currents and tempestuous seas often raging off the North Foreland.

It will be seen, therefore, that a lofty tower or lighthouse at Rutupiae would have been of the greatest value both for the guidance of friendly shipping and as a means of giving warning of the approach of the enemy.

The north wall of the *castrum* at Richborough is a remarkably perfect and interesting specimen of Roman masonry. It is noteworthy, too, as furnishing proof of the great care and thoroughness with which the Romans carried out their building works. At the base of the wall,

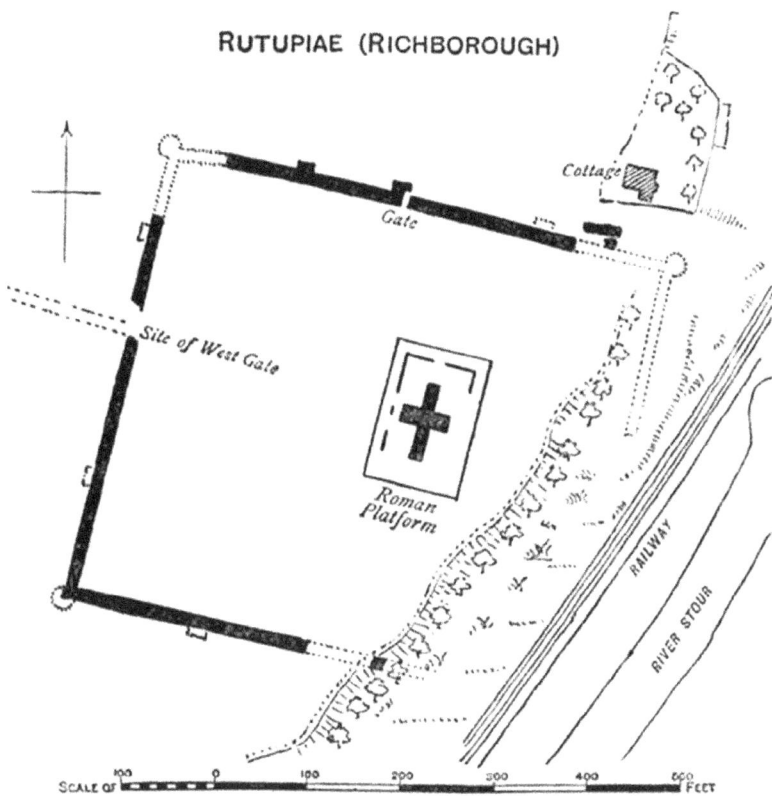

RUTUPIAE (RICHBOROUGH)

Cottage

Gate

Site of West Gate

Roman Platform

RAILWAY

RIVER STOUR

SCALE OF 100 0 100 200 300 400 500 FEET

FIG. 7. RUTUPIAE (RICHBOROUGH)

A Chapel converted into a Cottage
A House demolished by the Sea in 1781
Remains of a Tenter-Mill at Faversham
Isle of Sheppey

FIG. 8. RECULVER FROM A 1781 PRINT

on the outside, one sees four courses of flint in their natural form, and above them the following succession of materials, in ascending order: three courses of dressed flint; two courses of bonding tile; seven courses of *ashlar* and two of tile; seven courses of *ashlar* and two of tile; seven courses of *ashlar* and two of tile; seven courses of *ashlar* and two of tile; eight courses of *ashlar* and two of tile; nine courses of *ashlar*. The wall is 23 feet 2 inches high, and 10 feet 8 inches thick.

There is one aspect of some of the Roman coast fortresses which shows that their builders were not influenced entirely by utilitarian ideas. This is the methodical and tasteful use of stones of different colours in such a way as to produce a pleasing species of colour decoration. The aim obviously was to break up the monotony of broad spaces of masonry, and possibly, also, to enhance their apparent size by multiplication of detail. The north wall of Richborough, although to some extent marred by rebuilding of some part of it, affords an illustration of this. Here we find dark brownish-red ironstone built into the wall in a way which reminds one of bands of chequer work. A Pevensey again, where the stones are cut with the regularity and precision of brickwork, large blocks of similar sandstone are employed in regular order at different heights in the walls and bastions. To the latter in addition to their decorative use they serve to tie in the outer skin of masonry to the inner rubble.

6. DUBRIS, DOVER

A paper by Rev. Canon Puckle on Vestiges of Roman Dover was published some years ago in *Archaeologia Cantiana*.[8] It was accompanied by a plan in which are set out the outlines of what are supposed to have been the limits of the Roman town or fortress of Dover. Although the outline is merely tentative and hypothetical, there is a certain plausibility about the suggested site and size of the *castrum*. It was situated, as is pointed out, quite away from the *pharos*, in the lowest part of the town, the present Market Square being approximately in the middle of the enclosure. The plan is roughly a parallelogram with certain irregularities on the north-west angle.

On the top of the eastern and western heights of Dover a lighthouse was erected by the Romans for the guidance of ships into the narrow mouth of the river. Traces of that on the western heights still remain, or remained recently: whilst that on the eastern heights stands intact, one of the most remarkable and interesting pieces of Roman

---

8. Vol. xx, pp. 128-136.

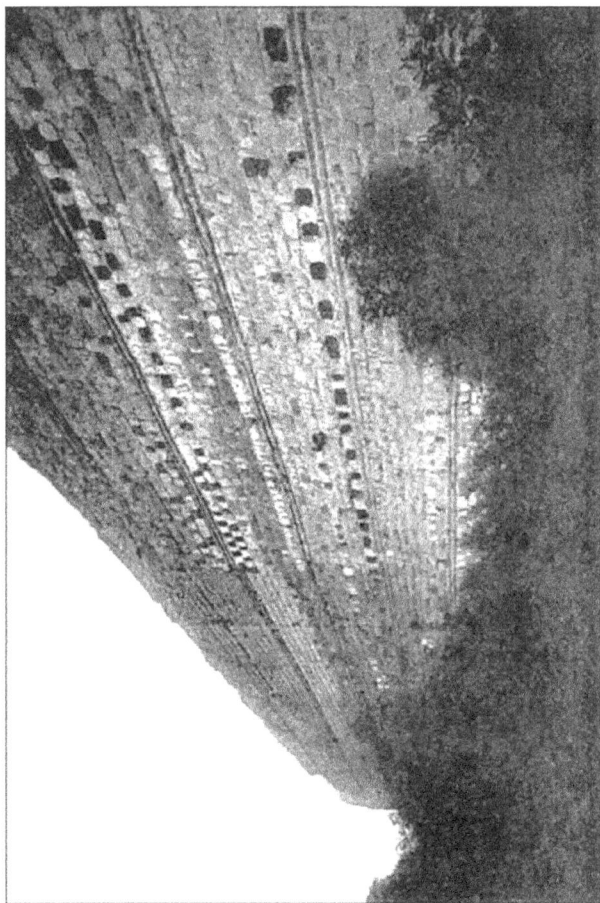

FIG. 9. RICHBOROUGH, KENT. EXTERIOR OF NORTH WALL

architecture now remaining in the kingdom.

The Roman *pharos* at Dover consists of a strong and massive tower, hollow within, which rises to a height of 42 feet, having walls whose thickness varies from 12 feet at the base to about 7 feet at the top. The structure is not entirely of Roman workmanship, because in the thirteenth century certain additions were made to its outer walls.

Doubtless its massive masonry was calculated to withstand the severe storms to which its exposed position on the lofty cliff subjected it. Whether employed for signalling purposes or as a lighthouse, this building was doubtless in such a position as to communicate with similar buildings on the coast of France, and with the lighthouse or signalling tower (it may have served in both capacities) at Richborough.

The *pharos* on the western heights of Dover, of which little now remains, must have formed an extremely valuable auxiliary to that on the eastern heights, affording a guide for ships making at night for the haven of Dover. It is not at all improbable that both structures combined the purposes of lighthouses at night with those of signalling stations in the daytime.

The precise details of the existing *pharos*, although of the greatest interest from architectural and archaeological points of view, are not necessary to our present purpose, but a few facts are worthy of notice.

The masonry throughout is of *tufa* with the exception of two or three courses of Roman tiles at intervals of about 4 feet, and the foundations, which again consist of several courses of tiles arranged in three sets-off, and with an octagonal plan.

The tower is of octagonal plan externally, and square within, where each of the four walls measures about 14 feet. The structure is believed to have been repaired and cased with flint in the year 1259, when Richard de Codnore was Constable of Dover Castle. His arms, Barry of six, argent and azure, are carved in stone on the north side of the *pharos*. The octagonal chamber in the top story of the tower appears to have been restored or rebuilt in Tudor times.

It is interesting and instructive to compare the Dover lighthouses in their relation to the French coast and Richborough, with the signalling tower or lighthouse of West Mersea, by means of which communications were kept up with the sea-coast station and *castrum* of Othona.

Bearing in mind the defensive character of the forts with which

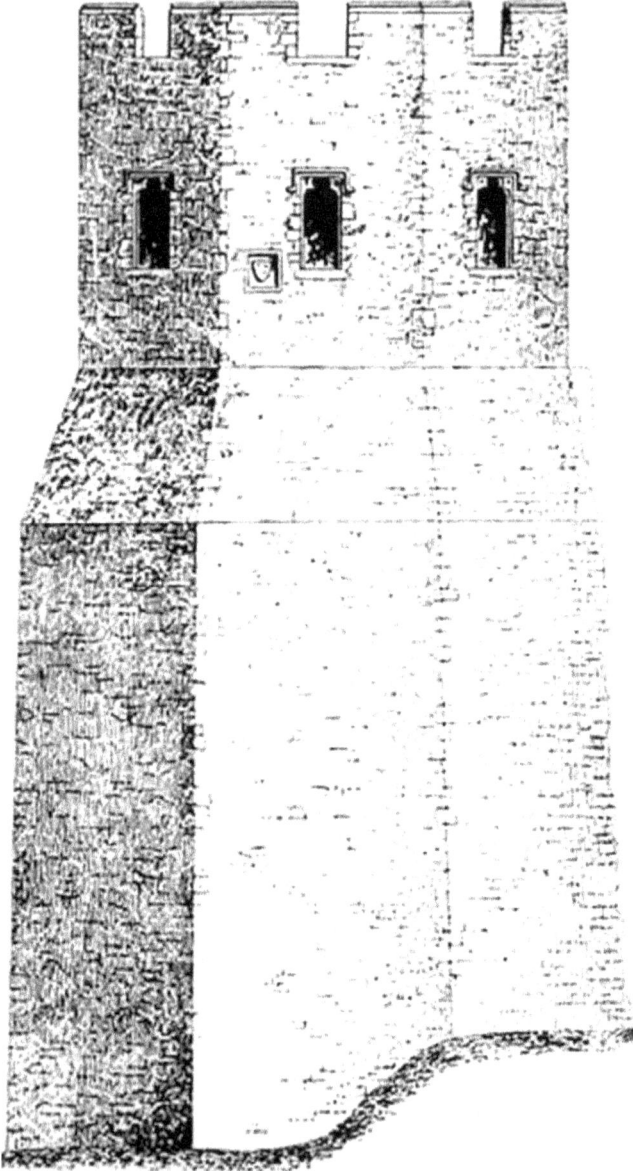

EXTERNAL ELEVATION ON THE NORTH SIDE

FIG. 10. PHAROS, DOVER

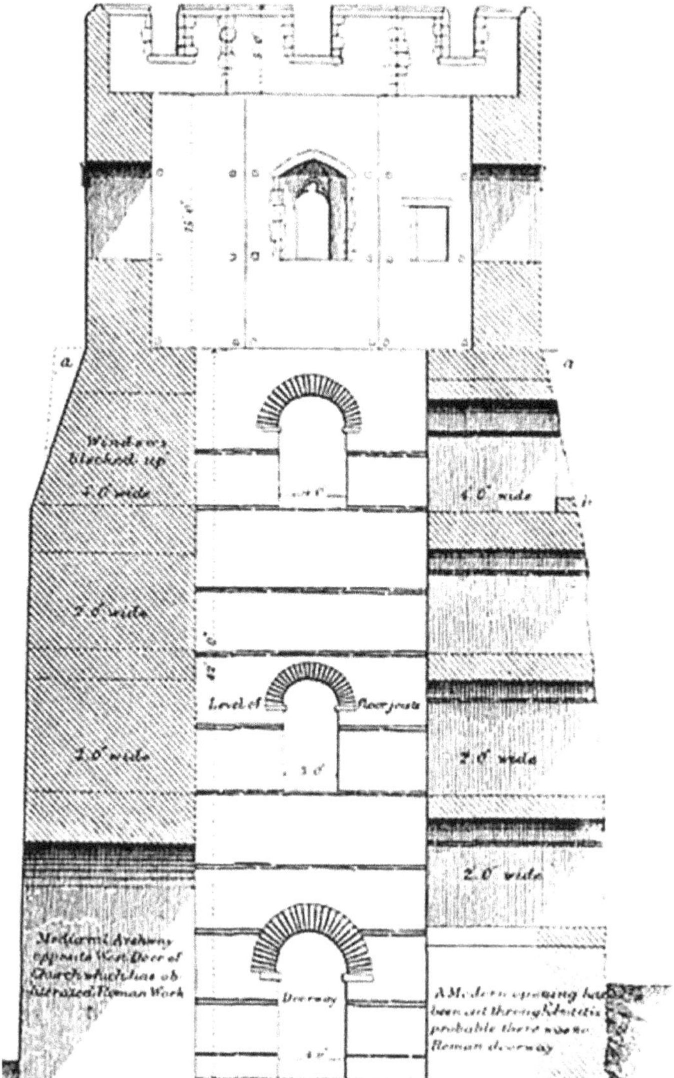

Windows
blocked up
2'0 wide

2'0 wide

2'0 wide

2'0 wide

2'0 wide

2'0 wide

Level of   floor joists

Modern Archway
opposite West Door of
Church which has obliterated Roman Work

Doorway

A Modern opening has
been cut through it: it is
probable there was no
Roman doorway

SECTION ON A B

FIG. 11. PHAROS, DOVER

the lighthouses were associated, it seems probable that their purpose had a close relation to the work of watching the coast, and obtaining early information of the approach of invaders.

There is a strong probability that more of such buildings for observing the approach of enemies once existed, traces of which have now perished.

7. PORTUS LEMANIS

Situated originally on the side of a spur of high ground at Lymne, near Hythe, and overlooking the flat ground of Romney Marsh, was a fortified station of sufficient importance to rank as a town. Its distance from Dover, and its situation on the south coast, suggest that it cannot have formed a part of the group of contemporary fortresses which defended the east coast of Kent.

Owing to a landslip on a large scale, which happened possibly before the Norman Conquest, the whole of the site upon which this town stood slipped downwards towards Romney Marsh, and the massive walls and towers by which it was once encompassed were disturbed, shattered, and overturned.

The form, as far as can be gathered from the disturbed foundations, was somewhat irregular. The east and west walls were parallel, and the south wall ran at right angles with them, but the north wall had an outward bow-like projection. The walls, when the place was intact, enclosed a space of about 11 acres, and were from 12 feet to 14 feet thick, whilst the height of both walls and mural towers was somewhat more than 20 feet.

The purpose of placing a strongly fortified town at this place was partly in order to command a view over the surrounding country, and partly to defend the Roman port which was situated on a branch of the River Limene,[9] or rather, just at the foot of the hill on the side of which it stood.

Among the discoveries made at Portus Lemanis there were two of remarkable and significant character. The first consisted of a mutilated altar-stone, bearing a much-worn inscription indicating the dedication of the altar by a *praefect* of the British fleet, named Aufidius Pantera, probably to Neptune. The stone was found built into the masonry of the principal gate, and from its worn condition, and the remains of barnacles which it still bore when found, it was justly inferred that

9. Now occupied by the Royal Military Canal constructed as part of the defence against Napoleon's threatened invasion.

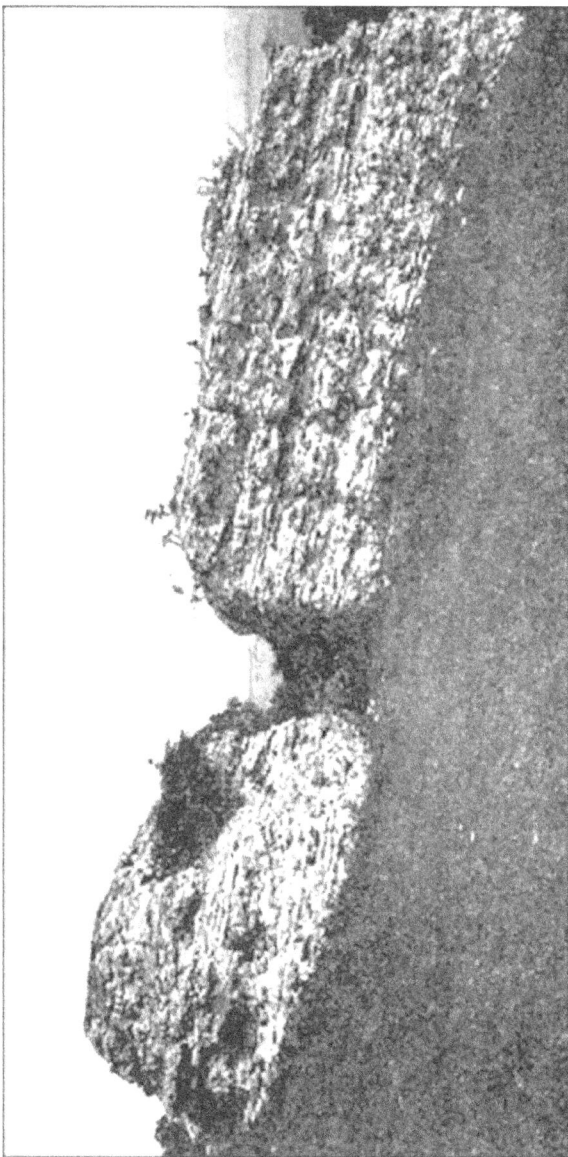

Fig. 12. Roman Walls, Lymne, Kent

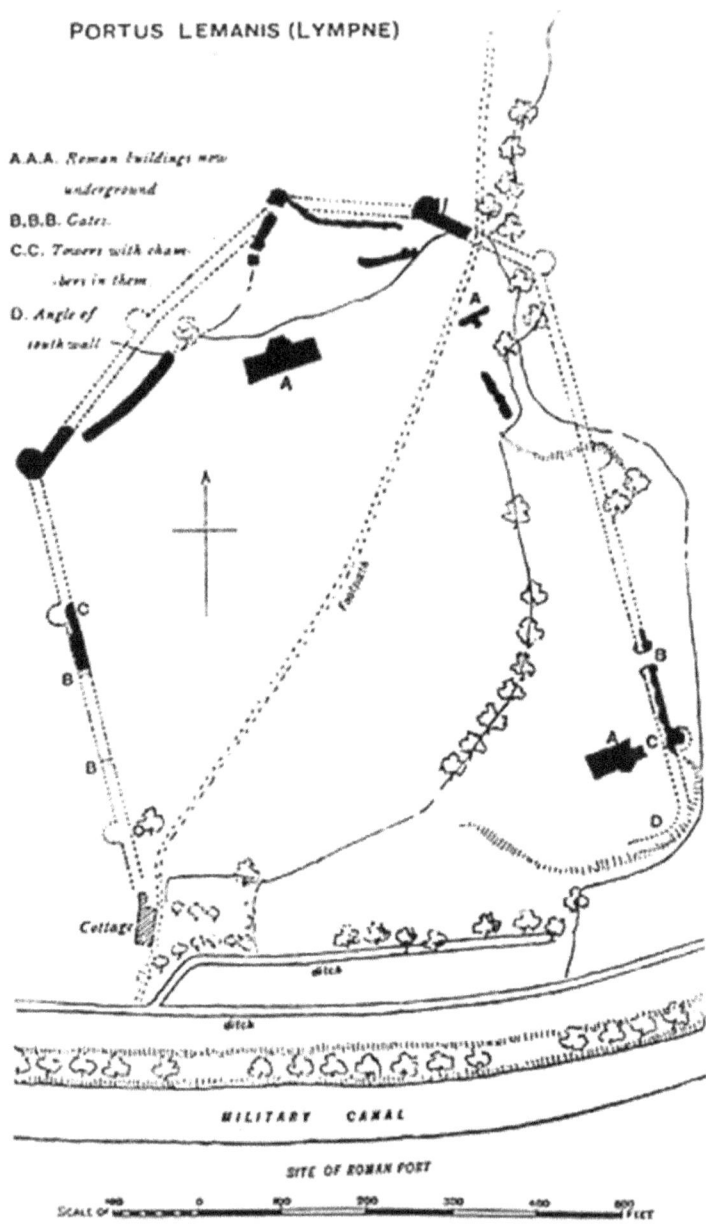

PORTUS LEMANIS (LYMPNE)

A.A.A. Roman buildings now underground
B.B.B. Gates
C.C. Towers with chambers in them
D. Angle of south wall

Cottage

ditch

ditch

MILITARY CANAL

SITE OF ROMAN PORT

SCALE OF FEET

FIG. 13. PORTUS LEMANIS (LYMPNE)

it belonged to an earlier period than that of the building of the gate. The second discovery, of quite equal interest with the first, was that of a number of broken roof and other tiles, inscribed CLBR, which has been read *Classiarii Britannici*, Marines of the British fleet.

From these discoveries one may gather that at some period, probably before that of Constantine, a division of the British fleet was situated at Portus Lemanis, and that some of the buildings there were erected by the crew from the fleet.

The principal gate, which may have been battered down during a siege, and required rebuilding, was evidently the work of a late date in the Roman period. This view is supported by a comparison of the whole building with the work at Anderida (Pevensey). The general arrangement of the walls, the disposition of the mural towers, or bastions, and the facing of regularly cut limestone blocks present points of very considerable similarity.

It will be observed from a comparison of Portus Lemanis with Anderida (about to be described) that there is reason to think that both works belong to a date somewhat late in the Roman period.

8. ANDERIDA (PEVENSEY)

The *castrum* at Pevensey retains so much of its enclosing walls and bastions that it is particularly worthy of study if one would learn, by direct observation, what splendid specimens of architecture the Romans erected in this country. Although a mediaeval castle has been built within the boundary of the Roman *castrum*, the walls of the latter may be traced for almost the whole of the circuit, and on the north, east, and west sides they stand to a considerable height. At the south-western extremity is the main gateway, its two flanking towers forming perhaps the most prominent features. Proceeding to the north of this gate we find three good specimens of bastions of somewhat horse-shoe form on plan. A series of six similarly planned bastions remain at the opposite side of the fortress, the general plan of which may be said to be elliptical.

The character of the facing masonry, especially on the south-west side, is quite remarkable. The facing consists of carefully squared blocks of limestone laid with the regularity and precision of brickwork.

Two characteristics stand out prominently in comparing this with other Roman *castra* on the coast of Britain. One is the irregularity of plan, the other is the presence of numerous projecting bastions. Both point to the lateness of the work, and some valuable evidence, con-

Fig. 14. Bastion on South-Western Wall, Pevensey

firming this view, has been brought to light in recent years. In 1907 Mr. Charles Dawson, F.S.A., communicated to the Society of Antiquaries [10] some notes on tiles found here bearing the stamp

HON AUG
ANDRIA

The first line apparently refers to the Emperor Honorius (395–423), whilst the second may be regarded as indicating with somewhat less certainty the name Anderida.

9. PORTUS MAGNUS (PORCHESTER)

This remarkably fine *castrum*, which stands on the edge of the most northern creek forming a part of Portsmouth Harbour, consists of a square enclosure containing a space of about 9 acres. Its walls, 10 feet in thickness, are constructed of flint rubble with courses of bonding-tiles. Originally each angle was furnished with a hollow bastion, or tower, and similar bastions, hollow within, were placed along the walls at intervals of from 100 feet to 200 feet. Some of these bastions have been destroyed, but fourteen examples, in a more or less perfect condition, remain. The water-gate, on the eastern side, still survives in a peculiarly perfect state. It is remarkable from the fact that the blocks of stone forming its semicircular arch are of light and dark colour, and are arranged alternately, so as to impart a picturesque and decorative effect.

The identification of Porchester with the Portus Magnus of the Romans has been questioned by Professor Haverfield, and there can be no doubt that it rests upon insufficient evidence. Conceivably it may be the Portus Adurni of the Romans: but this is not certain.

A Norman castle, with remarkably fine keep, still practically intact, was built in the north-west corner, and the parish church, also of Norman architecture, was constructed near the south-east angle, within the walls of the *castrum*.

Clausentum, an important Roman station, now known as Bitterne, is situated a little to the north of Southampton, on the banks of the tidal estuary of the River Itchen. Practically nothing in the shape of architectural traces now remain, but from accounts written before their complete destruction we know that it was enclosed with walls 9 feet thick, and constructed of flint bonded with large flat tiles and roughly faced with small square stones. It has been supposed that the

---

10. Proceedings, xxi, 410.

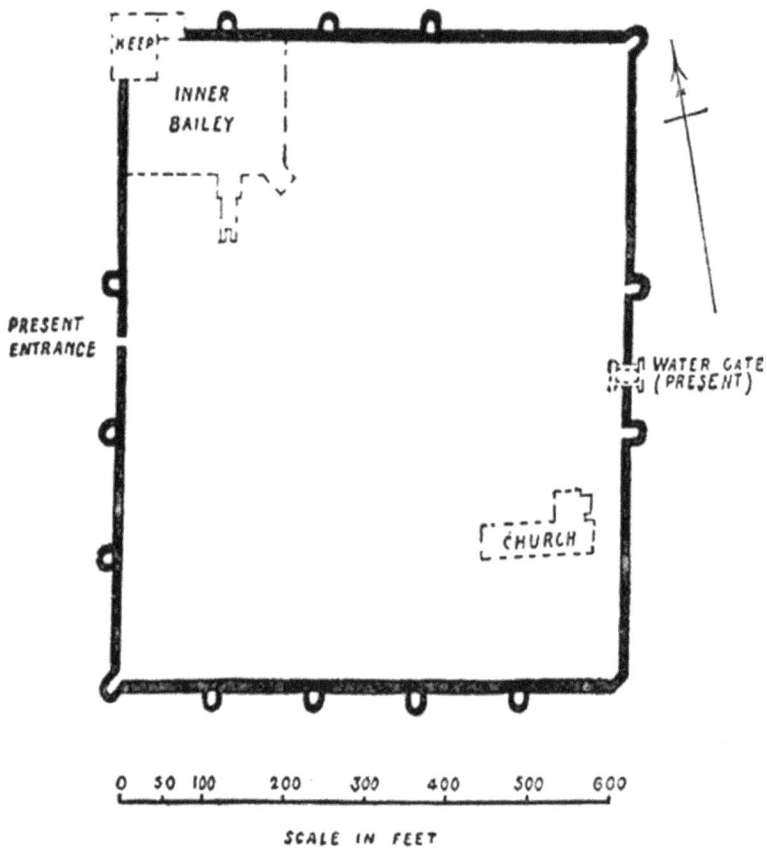

KEEP

INNER
BAILEY

PRESENT
ENTRANCE

WATER GATE
(PRESENT)

CHURCH

0 50 100   200   300   400   500   600

SCALE IN FEET

FIG. 15. PLAN OF PORCHESTER ROMAN CASTRUM

FIG. 16. THE WATER-GATE, PORCHESTER

outer defences when perfect measured 500 yards in length. The station was three-sided, the walls each having an outward curve. The outer defences are believed to have enclosed an area of 20 acres: the inner defences, 10 acres.

Cardiff.—Although not situated near the Continent, it is probable that Cardiff took its part in the defence of our coast during the Roman period. Whether the Roman fortress at this point formed part of the defences which were placed under the control of the Count of the Saxon Shore may be doubted, but in size and general plan it certainly resembled the coast fortresses of the south-eastern shores.

In the course of recent excavations in and near Cardiff Castle the nearly complete ground-plan of this castrum was found. Its form was nearly quadrangular, the only irregularity being in the western wall, which was inclined eastward at its southern end. Gates were situated about the middle of the northern and southern walls, whilst semi-circular bastions were placed along the walls at intervals, roughly, of about 120 feet. At the angles were built towers of irregular form and of somewhat unusual interest, from the fact that they were obviously additions to the original work. The area enclosed by the walls was roughly a square of 600 feet.

The question of angle-towers or bastions is one of considerable importance. Their presence in a Roman *castrum* may generally be taken as evidence of late date; but it is necessary to bear in mind that in some cases they have certainly been added to give strength to fortresses of early type, which, as we have seen in the cases of Reculver and Brancaster, were furnished with rounded angles, without any such projecting features as angle-towers or bastions. At Cardiff [11] it is perfectly clear that the original building had rounded angles against which towers of irregularly circular plan were subsequently built.

As at Pevensey and Porchester, a Norman castle was ingeniously constructed within this *castrum* by placing the mound towards the north-western corner. Two walls thrown out from this, one towards the western wall and the other to about the middle of the southern wall, enclosed practically a quarter of the whole area in the south-western angle, and formed the inner court, whilst the whole of the rest of the area of the castrum formed the outer court. It is obvious that at the period when this Norman castle was built the Roman walls were sufficiently perfect to afford an effective barrier of defence.

---

11. *Archaeologia*, lvii, 335-352.

FIG. 17. PORCHESTER. EXTERIOR OF WEST WALL

The coast to the north of Brancaster, the most northern of the nine regular Roman coast *castra*, is provided in certain places with defences of Roman date, either in the form of watch-houses, or light-houses, or fortresses.

Professor Haverfield, in a recent lecture on the subject, [12] suggests that such structures once existed at (1) Huntcliffe (near Saltburn); (2) at a point near Staithes; (3) on the high promontory of Peak, near Robin Hood Bay; and (4) on another high headland, called Carrnase, to the north of Filey Bay. Generally speaking, the altitude of the sites of these works suggests their use for watching or lighting purposes rather than for purely military defence.

To a certain extent the Roman walled towns of Canterbury, Rochester, Chichester, Colchester, and London, must be regarded as having exercised a share in the coast defence of England, because they were situated on rivers now or formerly navigable, and not too far from the sea-coast to be absolutely without value in repelling invaders.

The fact that they were constructed specially for defensive purposes, not only against near neighbours, but also against those unwelcome visitors who, from the remote past, and all through the middle ages, have been attracted by the wealth of England, brings them within the scope of the present essay. For obvious reasons, however, and mainly because of the question of space, it is unnecessary to describe in detail every defensive work which was partially available for English coast defence.

---

12. "Notes on the Roman Coast Defences of Britain, especially in Yorkshire" (*Journal of Roman Studies*, ii, 201-214).

PART 2

Saxon, Danish and Norman Occupation

The Saxon Settlement of England

With the settlement of the Saxons, the Angles, and the Jutes in England, this book has no immediate concern, but it is worthy of note that having driven the British people westward into Wales and south-westward into Cornwall, they quickly spread over the greater part of England. Their weapons, their costumes, their jewellery, and, indeed, their general standard of civilization, are clearly reflected and illustrated by the contents of numerous cemeteries, which have been scientifically explored and examined. We know little of their houses or other buildings until the eleventh century, when we are aided by the actual remains of churches, the evidence of illuminated manuscripts and the *Anglo-Saxon Chronicle.*

There is, however, one fact which stands out quite clearly in an age which is remarkable for the obscurity of its historical evidence. This is that the Saxons, as a general rule, did not immediately occupy the ruins of Romano-British towns or houses. On the contrary, they seem to have avoided them, even to the extent of diverting the roads which originally passed through the towns. This is so marked that we can only infer that it was due to a superstitious dread of sites which had once been inhabited by the Romans. The site of the important Romano-British town of Silchester, although full of evidences of Roman occupation, and of intercourse with contemporary British population, has furnished absolutely no trace of Saxon habitation.

What was true of cities and towns and houses, was probably true of the coast fortresses upon which the Romans, particularly in the latter part of their occupation of Britain, had expended so much time and labour.

It is extremely doubtful whether the Saxons ever garrisoned the coast fortresses abandoned when the Roman legions were withdrawn from Britain. Numismatic evidence shows that there was an Anglo-Saxon mint at Lymne, the Portus Lemanus of the Romans, and possessing an important harbour. The coins minted there range from King Edgar's time to that of Edward the Confessor, but there is reason to believe that the Roman site was deserted at an early period in the Saxon occupation, the neighbouring town of Hythe taking its place. Certain Saxon coins bearing the legend RIC, have been attributed to a mint at Richborough, but there is a good deal of doubt as to this identification. Coins of middle and late Saxon kings, as we might have expected, were minted at Canterbury, Rochester, Sandwich, and Dover, but generally speaking the evidence of Saxon coinage does not support the view that the purely coast fortresses of the Romans were ever used to any great extent by the Saxons.

The Saxons built *burhs*, or towns fortified with earthen ramparts, probably palisaded, in many parts of the kingdom, and the evidence for them will be found in the *Anglo-Saxon Chronicle*, but they were not castle-builders. They were a people with tribal instincts and traditions. They did not construct defensive dwellings for a single lord and his family and retainers; they expended their efforts rather on fortified towns for the protection of all their people.

Wareham, in Dorset, is generally believed to be an example of the fortified towns of the Anglo-Saxons. Sandwich, again, which retains considerable traces of mediaeval earthen ramparts, and was a port of great consequence in early times, was also probably fortified by the Anglo-Saxons. It is impossible to say whether any part of its earthwork defences are of that early period. Dover, Canterbury, Rochester, Chichester, Colchester, and some other walled towns of Roman origin, appear, from archaeological evidence, to have had Anglo-Saxon populations, possibly of late date, when the Roman houses had disappeared and the dread of the Romans had become forgotten. It may be doubted whether the Saxons took advantage of the Roman walled defences.

As we have already pointed out, there are very few remains of purely defensive works belonging to the Anglo-Saxon period. For this reason the quadrangular moated site at Bayford, near Sittingbourne, in Kent, is of peculiar interest, because as Mr. Harold Sands, F.S.A.,[1] has pointed out, the *Anglo-Saxon Chronicle* mentions that King Alfred here threw up a *geweorc* in 893 in order to repel the inroads of the Danes under Bjorn-laernside, who had formed an encampment at a

1. *Memorials of Old Kent.*

place called Milton, in Kemsley Downs on the opposite side of Milton Creek, a mile and a half north of Bayford Castle.

The incursions of the Danes and other raiders provided the Saxons with excellent opportunities for displaying their skill in defensive warfare, and brought into prominence a great man whose name must ever be held in honour as one of the bravest and most enlightened defenders of our shores. To King Alfred, commonly known in recent years as Alfred the Great, belongs the credit of having conceived the idea of destroying the enemy's power at sea in order to secure the safety of our shores. He seems to have been the first man in our history to have grasped this great principle. He led this navy to action in person and so acquired the epithet of "the first English admiral."

Early in his reign, King Alfred devoted his attention to the important question of his navy, and he brought it to such a condition of strength and proficiency as to defeat the Danish raiders, one of the greatest pests by which our shores were ever troubled.

Danish Incursions and Camps

The coast-line of England is of curious complexity, and is long out of all proportion to that of any other great European nation, perhaps not even excepting Norway. Consequently its defence presents and always has presented problems of great difficulty. Much of the coast-line is rocky and dangerous even for friendly shipping. In other places, where cliffs are absent, shoals and sand-banks make navigation and landing difficult and dangerous. In looking back to the days when there were no artificial harbours and landing-places, one sees quite clearly that estuaries of rivers would have afforded the safest and most convenient places for landing. That such spots were selected is abundantly proved by tradition, history, and actual contemporary remains.

The Danes were quick to seize upon such favourable landing-places. They were provided with boats of great length and slight draught, and their operations were not limited, therefore, to the deeper rivers. During the latter years of the eighth century, and practically throughout the tenth, the Danish raids on Britain were numerous. In due course they established themselves on river-banks, and built permanent camps. According to the *Anglo-Saxon Chronicle*, Hasting constructed and occupied a camp at Shoebury for a short period in the year 894. The camp, or such part of it as now exists, has been described by Mr. Spurrell [2] as a Danish work. The place has been much

---

2. *Archaeological Journal*, xlvii, 78-81.

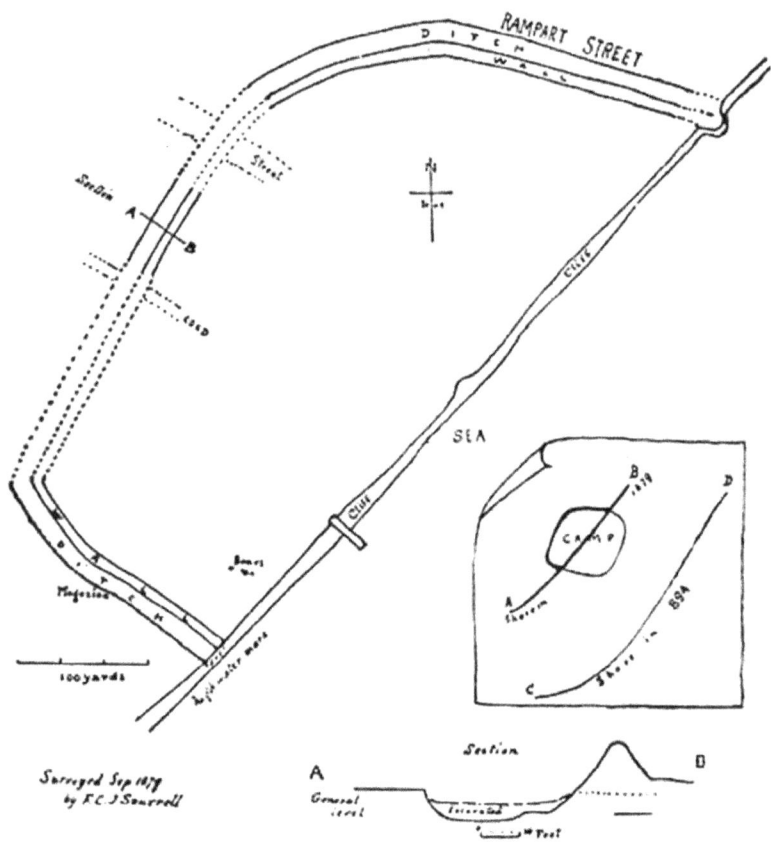

FIG. 18. PLAN OF DANISH CAMP, SHOEBURY, ESSEX

destroyed by the inroads of the sea and the building of various military works, such as barracks, etc., but the plan can be made out, and as restored by Mr. Spurrell, may be described as an irregular quadrangle with rounded corners, and containing an area of about one third part of a square mile.

Another Danish camp was constructed the same year at Appledore, the Danes sailing or rowing up the river Rother. According to Somner[3] they discovered at Appledore a half-built fortress, but finding it insufficient for their needs they built a larger entrenchment on the same site.

Other places where the Danes settled were Benfleet, probably Swanscombe (although the existing remains of the camp belong probably to the Norman period); Bramber, Sussex; an earthwork surrounding East Mersea Church, Essex; and many other places. Here they constructed their camps and established their forces for long periods, using the adjacent rivers as channels for quickly putting to sea in their swiftly-moving boats when embarking on raiding excursions to the neighbouring coasts.

They raided Sheppey in 832, Kent, Canterbury and London in 851. In 876 they took Wareham, where are interesting earthen town-walls, perhaps of Saxon origin. During one or more of their raids in the Medway they penetrated as far as Rochester, which they pillaged. Sandwich and Canterbury suffered much from their visits in the eleventh century.

It may be noted that the favourite methods of the Danes when invading England was to enter the rivers so as to reach by that means populous towns and districts where they could seize valuable possessions. The monastic houses were their favourite prey, and few in England escaped injury or pillage at their hands.

The following extract from the *Anglo-Saxon Chronicle* gives a vivid picture of the doings of the Danes at the end of the tenth century:

A.D. 999. In this year the army again came about into the Thames, and then went up along the Medway, and to Rochester. And then the Kentish force came against them, and they stoutly engaged together, but alas! that they too quickly gave way and fled; because they had not the support which they should have had. And the Danish had possession of the place of carnage; and then took horses and rode whithersoever

<hr>

3. *Roman Ports.*

they themselves would, and ruined and plundered almost all the West Kentish. Then the king with his 'witan' resolved that they should be opposed with a naval force, and also with a land force. But when the ships were ready, then they delayed from day to day, and harassed the poor people who lay in the ships; and ever as it should be forwarder, so was it later, from one time to another: and ever they let their foes' army increase, and ever they receded from the sea, and ever they went forth after them. And then in the end neither the naval force nor the land force was productive of anything but the people's distress, and a waste of money, and the emboldening of their foes.

The Norman Invasion of England

It is a remarkable fact that the greatest event in the whole history of foreign attack upon England, namely, the invasion under the leadership of William, Duke of Normandy, in 1066, excited less interest, and provoked less effective opposition than many other incidents of infinitely minor importance.

The invasion was not unexpected by any means. When tidings of the projected invasion reached England, the largest fleet and army ever seen in this country were being mobilized at Sandwich. Yet, when the Norman invaders actually arrived the English made practically no opposition at all. It appears that the crews of the navy were tired of being under arms so long, and went home; whilst the king was bound to go northward to put down the troubles in Yorkshire. Nothing was ready.

The Norman fleet consisted, according to various accounts, of from 696 to 1,000 vessels. It can hardly be described as a navy, because the ships were too small to carry much more than the men and their arms: there was no room for provisions, and when on the 28 September 1066, the invaders landed in Pevensey Bay they encountered no opposition. In the Battle of Hastings the English forces were protected within palisaded entrenchments, but the result of the conflict was a decisive defeat.

The Normans having secured a foothold in the country, commenced at once to make their tenure secure, and to establish their power. This they accomplished with wonderful skill and success.

Norman Coast Castles

The castles first built in England by the Normans consisted of palisaded earthworks, the main feature being a lofty but truncated mound encircled by a deep ditch, and closely related to it were generally two courts or baileys. They were built in such situations as would command rivers and important roads, and so dominate the English people. Usually the castles of this period were built just within the boundaries of walled towns. The relation of the Tower to the City of London affords an excellent example of this arrangement.

Primarily the purpose of the Norman castle was to complete the work begun at the Battle of Hastings of subjugating the native population of England, and it is believed that castles of this type were employed for this purpose, because of the ease and rapidity with which they could be thrown up. Castles of this type were erected in England, not only after the Norman Conquest but also before it, and at one time the idea was generally held that they represented the usual and normal species of defence employed in Saxon times. The late G. T. Clark, who was a pioneer in the scientific study of English and Welsh castles, considered that these works were the actual *burhs* of the Anglo-Saxons, so often mentioned in the *Anglo-Saxon Chronicle*.

The theory was generally accepted for some years, but in due course doubts were cast upon it by the researches of Dr. J. Horace Round, Mrs. E. S. Armitage and others. It is now generally held that those examples of this type of defence which are known to have been constructed before the Conquest were built under the influence of Edward the Confessor's Norman friends. England at that time was following the fashions of Normandy; but the great majority of defences of this type were built, probably, very soon after the Norman Conquest, and under the direct influence of the Norman Conquerors. It is worthy of note that numerous examples exist to this day in Normandy, and some, with the characteristic palisaded mound, are represented in the Bayeux tapestry.

In many cases the earthwork castles as first built were, in due course, rebuilt in stone, the top of the mound being capped by a shell-keep and the other eminences being surmounted and reinforced by walls. Another type of keep, generally square in plan and of great strength and size, was built, as at Dover, Rochester, Canterbury, London, etc.; but such massive structures required firm foundations, and they were always built on undisturbed sites. These two kinds of keeps practically determine the two types into which the Norman castles built in England naturally fall.

A fairly large proportion of those Norman castles which may be considered to have been built for coast defence, have been constructed in such a way as to take advantage of pre-existing Roman *castra*. Porchester is an admirable specimen. Here the north-western portion of the Roman enclosure has been cut off by Norman walls so as to form the inner bailey, whilst the remainder has been converted into the outer bailey. Pevensey, London, Rochester, Colchester, Cardiff and Lancaster are other excellent examples.

In passing, it may be noted, that at Reculver and Porchester, the parish church has been built, doubtless for safety, within the walls of the *castrum*; whilst at Pevensey two parish churches have been erected sufficiently near the *castrum* to suggest that the sites were selected with a view to securing protection.

The regular castles of masonry erected during the reign of Henry II, a great castle-building period, although very important as military works, were not in the main built for the defence of the coast. But it is necessary to bear in mind that in ancient times river-courses, even far from the sea-coast, were subject in a peculiar degree to the incursions of the enemy, and the great Norman keeps of Canterbury, Rochester, and the White Tower of London, although situated far from the sea-coast, played an important part in the defence of the coast. At Porchester, Pevensey, Hastings, Folkestone and Dover, the relation between the Norman castles and the coast defences was much more intimate.

PART 3

Mediaeval Castles and Walled Towns on the Coast

In the following account of the more important of the castles which in mediaeval times guarded the coast, it has been found convenient to include a notice of those walled towns with which, in many cases, they were closely associated. The mediaeval castle, generally speaking, represents an effort to maintain the power of the feudal lord, and, in a lesser and secondary degree, provision for resisting raids and invasion by foreign enemies. Walled towns, on the other hand, when situated on or near the coasts, or on navigable rivers, were primarily designed for coast defence. The mediaeval castles which were built in situations remote from the coast were the fastnesses and strongholds of nobles fighting amongst themselves or against the king.

In the following accounts of the more important examples of castles and walled towns wholly or partially designed for the defence of the coast, occasion will be taken to point out the interesting series of developments through which these mediaeval fortifications passed as time went on. For example:

The massive keep of the Norman castles was able to resist fire and battering-ram when the besieging force came near enough to apply them. Its strength consisted in its thick walls, its height, and its massive masonry. The Edwardian castle, on the other hand, presents certain structural improvements which mark a great advance in military construction. The walls, gates, and towers are so built as to present curved surfaces to the engines of the enemy, with the result that missiles hurled against them would glance off at various angles according to the direction of the curve at the point of impact. The extent to which this development of the curve is carried in the walls of many of the Edwardian castles is quite remarkable and instructive. It shows that mere weight and bulk were no longer relied upon, but constructive skill and the judicious use of materials were guiding principles in the military architecture of the period.

The following list does not include the sixteenth century block-houses and other fortifications erected by Henry VIII, and in subsequent years.

The defences on the eastern coast of England consist of an extremely interesting and important series of fortresses. In the extreme north is—

Berwick-upon-Tweed.—A town which, from its position on the English and Scottish border, has always been a place of strategic moment, and which Queen Elizabeth spoke of as "the chief key of the realm." In the time of Edward I (1272-1307) it was encompassed by a great moat, or ditch, 80 feet wide and 40 feet deep. A crenulated wall *from* 15 to 22 feet high, with 19 towers at intervals, was constructed during the reign of Edward II (1307-1327). A castle had been erected at Berwick during the reign of Henry II, and together with the Edwardian wall and ditch must have formed an extremely formidable defence.

The mediaeval fortifications included a large area, and in the time of Elizabeth a portion within this area was enclosed and strengthened by works of more modern character, the main features of which comprised five examples of the orillon type of bastion. The orillon was an enclosure of flattened triangular form, projecting beyond the curtain. The middle angle was obtuse, and the passage from the opening in the curtain into the bastion was somewhat restricted. It is obvious that such a bastion as this, which was introduced into England in the latter half of the sixteenth century, would give the maximum range for defensive fire, whilst affording most valuable means of protecting the flanks.

The fortifications of Berwick-upon-Tweed were primarily intended for defence against the Scottish Border raiders and incursions coming overland, but they also served to protect the town against the enemy approaching by sea.

Bamborough.—The site of this castle must have been a place of great natural strength, and probably a fortress, from prehistoric times downwards. It would not be inaccurate to describe it as one of the important and historic spots in the kingdom. The castle dates from a period before the Norman Conquest. Here the Danish raiders were successfully repelled in 912. The castle was maintained in a good state of defence under Henry I, and the keep is of the twelfth century. Structural repairs were made at frequent intervals, *viz.*, in 1183, 1197, 1198, 1201, and 1202. A new gatehouse was built here in consequence of the invasions of the Scots in 1383-4.

On several occasions Bamborough Castle has served as a prison, and it was brought into considerable prominence during the Wars of the Roses. The part it played in the various wars between England and Scotland must have been important. [1]

Dunstanburgh.—Situated on a bold, rugged headland, this fine castle reminds one of such great fortresses on the east coast as Scarborough and Tynemouth. Its share in the Border troubles was perhaps less than that of Bamborough. Dunstanburgh is the largest castle in Northumberland, is built on a remarkable plan, and comprises an area of ten acres, the main part of which was occupied by the outer bailey. Its history is associated with Simon de Montfort and Thomas of Lancaster.

The castle was mainly erected in 1313-14. The great gatehouse of the latter part of the fourteenth century, was planned and built on a colossal scale, and still forms a striking object, even in its ruin. By the sixteenth century the place had fallen into ruin. [2]

Warkworth.—This castle, remarkable for its eccentric plan, was built about the middle of the twelfth century.

Tynemouth.—The priory and castle of Tynemouth (for it was a combination of both) occupied a prominent position among the mediaeval coast defences of England. The office of Prior of Tynemouth was one of great importance. The person who held it was possessed of vast spiritual and worldly influence. He maintained his own armed force, just as the Bishop of Durham did, and the gatehouse [3] of the priory was in reality a military fortress, a building of great solidity and strength. It was approached by a barbican, the passage-way being vaulted and furnished with a gate at each end. [4]

Scarborough.—This place was defended by walls or earthworks and a fosse before the time of Henry III. Its castle was built as early as the time of Stephen, and rebuilt or enlarged in the reign of Henry II.

---

1. *Northumberland County History*, i.
2. *Northumberland County History*, ii.
3. Built in 1390.
4. *Northumberland County History*, viii; *Archaeological Journal*, lxvii, 1-50.

During the Civil War Scarborough Castle was besieged. It was surrendered in 1645, and has long been in ruins. It enclosed nineteen acres of land and occupied a romantic site 300 feet above sea-level.

Hull.—From an early period this seaport has been defended by fortifications. In the seventeenth century these comprised a moat and a complete system of walls, fortified gates, and drawbridges. It possessed five gates, called Hessle Gate, Myton Gate, Beverley Gate, Low Gate, and North Gate, and two sally-ports. The whole fortified walls were 2,610 yards, or slightly less than one-and-a-half miles in circuit. In front of the principal gates were drawbridges and half-moon shaped batteries. In the year 1540 the eastern side of the town was defended by two blockhouses, erected by Henry VIII. These were known as the North Blockhouse and the South Blockhouse, and both mounted guns when the town was besieged during the Civil War. A castle was also built on the eastern side of the town by Henry VIII.

King's Lynn.—The eastern side of this important town was in former times defended by a wall strengthened by nine bastions, and by a broad and deep fosse over which were three drawbridges leading to the principal gates. One of the latter and fragments of the wall remain. From the statement of Stow in his *Chronicle*, and from certain illustrations of the walls as they existed in 1800, we may infer that the walls at any rate belonged to the first half of the thirteenth century. The East Gate and the West Gate were rebuilt on the sites of earlier gates in the fifteenth century.

Yarmouth.—The town-wall, of which some traces remain, measured between six and seven thousand feet in compass, and possessed ten gates and sixteen towers. Swinden, [5] the historian of Yarmouth, states that the building of the wall:

> Was begun on the east side, and very probably at the north-east tower in St. Nicholas's churchyard, and so proceeded southward: for in the 11th of Edward III we find them at work at the Black Friars, at the south end of the town; and afterwards we trace them to the north end, which, I presume, was the last part that was finished.
> And there is a tradition, that the north gate was built by the person or persons who had amassed considerable sums of mon-

---

5. *The History and Antiquities of the Ancient Burgh of Great Yarmouth*, by Henry Swinden, 1772.

58

Fig. 19. North Gate, Yarmouth, 1807

Fig. 20. South Gate, Yarmouth, 1807

ey by being employed in burying the dead in the time of the plague.

As soon as the walls were finished, there was made a moat or ditch round the town, with bridges at each gate: the whole so complete that boats could pass with their lading to any part of the town, for the conveniency of trade and commerce. And so careful were the magistrates to preserve the said moat from being filled or stopped with earth, rubbish, stones, etc., that in the rolls of the leets, there appear several fines, levied on different persons for offending in that behalf. Thus the tower being fortified with a wall and moat, towers, gates, and bars, was deemed a sufficient defence against all assailants with bows and arrows, slings, battering-rams, and all other missive engines of those times. But afterwards, when great guns of various denominations were employed in sieges, the aforesaid fortification, it was adjudged, would make but little resistance against them, without several additional works, as mounts, ravelins, etc.

In the 36th year of Henry VIII the fortifications of Yarmouth were strengthened by rampiring, or backing up the walls by earthwork mounds. Additional works were constructed by Queen Mary in 1557, and by Queen Elizabeth, the complete process of rampiring not having been finished until 1587, the year before the coming of the Spanish armada. In the following year it was considered desirable to secure the haven against any sudden attacks of the enemy, and it was accordingly decided to construct jetties of timber on either side of the entrance, whilst across the actual entrance was placed a boom of massive timbers furnished with iron spikes, and this was so constructed that it could be opened or closed at pleasure. This work, including probably the two jetties and the boom, cost £120.

Traces of the wall of Yarmouth and its towers still remain, whilst other evidence of the wall is the extraordinary way in which the houses are crowded together, leaving only narrow alleys, or "rows," for the traffic. A plan of Yarmouth in 1819, published as a frontispiece to John Preston's "Picture of Yarmouth," shows in an admirable way the congested state of the buildings within the walls.

Ipswich.—There is a tradition that Ipswich was defended by a wall and fortified gates soon after the time of the Norman Conquest, but unfortunately no traces of either remain. Westgate Street preserves the memory of the picturesque West Gate. The interesting old engraving

Fig. 21. St. Matthew's Gate, Ipswich From a 1785 print

FIG. 22. ORFORD CASTLE, SUFFOLK, 1810

shows St. Matthew's Gate, now demolished. There appears to have been a castle at Ipswich built by William the Conqueror, and Roger Bigot, one of the Conqueror's powerful nobles, held it. With the exception of certain earthworks all traces of the castle have perished. The form of the town in mediaeval times has been made out by John Wodderspoon in his *Memorials of Ipswich*, 1850.

Orford.—This castle, situated half a mile from the River Ore, in Suffolk (hence its name), commands a view of the sea, two miles distant, owing to the fact that it is built on a mound partly natural and partly artificial. All round is swampy ground.

The building of Orford Castle was begun in 1166. Strictly speaking, perhaps, it should not be called a castle: it was essentially a keep, and its purpose primarily was to serve as an outpost for observation and for the protection of the coast. The plan of the actual keep, if so we may term it, was peculiar, being circular within, and so much modified by the buttresses without as to present the appearance of a large number of angles.

Harwich.—This ancient seaport situated on the extreme north-eastern point of Essex has always been a place of some strategic importance. It formerly was encompassed by a wall which had four gates and three posterns. In addition Harwich once possessed a small castle and other fortifications, but owing to the inroads of the sea these have for many years been submerged. Traces of the walls or foundations of the castle were seen, however, in 1784, when an unusually low tide laid bare more than usual of the sea-bottom.

On the south side of the town are some ancient earthworks locally ascribed to the Romans, although upon slender evidence.

Colchester.—which is situated on the river Colne, and perhaps not too far from the shore to take some part in the defence of the coast, has been in its time a place of great importance and of formidable strength. Its walls, of which considerable parts remain, are of Roman workmanship, and its castle, built largely of Roman materials, and therefore by some regarded as Roman in date, is almost unquestionably of Norman construction. It must be admitted, however, that the castle presents several features which differentiate it from the normal castles of the Norman period. Originally the walls were furnished with four principal gates, *viz*.: Head Gate, North Gate, East Gate, and St. Botolph's or South Gate, and three posterns, viz.: West Postern in St. Mary's Street, Schere Gate or South Postern, and Rye Gate or

River Postern, but these have been demolished. The north and west sides of the town were defended by strong earthworks. The place was besieged for eleven weeks during the Civil War. It was held by the Royalist party, and on its fall, two of its most gallant defenders, Sir Charles Lucas and Sir George Lisle, were shot under the castle walls.

The weakness of mediaeval castles, built merely for passive resistance, has frequently been noticed, and what is true of them is equally true of the mediaeval walled town. Forces shut up within walls are obviously unable to prevent an enemy from over-running a country. It must be borne in mind, however, that the purpose of fortifications behind walls was not, and never has been, merely intended to oppose the ravages of the enemy. In that part of our military history which is subsequent to the use of gunpowder, the uses of walled defence has been varied and manifold. For example: they were intended to check the enemy's advance; to give time for mobilization; to protect the strategical disposition of the army, especially in the early stages of a campaign; to protect important junctions in the lines of communications; and to safeguard magazines and stores against sudden and surprise attack of the enemy.

Cowling.—The castle at Cowling or Cooling, situated about seven miles to the east of Gravesend, and just two from the sea-shore, was built between 1380 and 1385 by John de Cobham. The gatehouse, built in the regular form in vogue during the latter end of the fourteenth century, and comparable with that at Saltwood Castle and the West Gate of Canterbury, still remains in good preservation, as well as a good deal of the walls and angle-towers enclosing the inner ward, and certain parts of the walling enclosing the outer ward. The gatehouse just referred to is on the south side of the outer ward, to which it gives access.

Perhaps one of the most interesting things about Cowling Castle is the fact that it was built expressly for the defence of the coast against the French and the Spanish. This fact is rather pointedly referred to in the following contemporary inscription enamelled on copper plates attached to the eastern side of the gatehouse:

Knouweyth that beth and schul be
That i am mad in help of the cuntre
In knowyng of whych thyng
This is chartre and wytnessyng.

The inscription is set out in the form of a regular charter, to which

Fig. 23. Cowling Castle, Kent, 1784

is attached a seal bearing the Cobham arms, gules, on a chevron or, three lions rampant sable.

The situation of Cowling Castle on low-lying ground near the coast is a circumstance which confirms the idea that the fortress was built for coast defence purposes. On the other hand, however, inscriptions of this kind are of great rarity, and it has been suggested with great show of reason, that whilst the purpose was partly for the defence of the coast and partly to keep the people of Kent in order in what were peculiarly troubled times, the inscription was so worded as to divert attention from the latter. The suggestion is worthy of consideration, but the fact remains that towards the end of the fourteenth century this part of Kent was overrun by Frenchmen and Spaniards, who burned and destroyed all the houses they came across, and Cobham's intention in building Cowling Castle was to check these incursions.

Rochester.—It is clear that Rochester has in its time been an important part of our coast defences. It still retains many fragments of its Roman wall, whilst its Norman castle is represented mainly by a stately keep 70 feet square in plan, and 113 feet in height, which forms an impressive object, and is in fact a remarkably fine example of castle-building. The Norman keep was built between the years 1126 and 1139. The city wall, which was built in places on the site of the Roman wall, dates from the year 1225.

Queenborough.—There is a tradition, possibly it is little more, that a residence of the Anglo-Saxon kings of Kent was situated here near the north-western mouth of the Swale, the building being afterwards known as the castle of Sheppey, in which island it is situated. The whole fortress was rebuilt by Edward III about the year 1361 according to plans made by William of Wykeham. Edward III in due course visited the place and gave it the name of Queenborough in honour of his queen Philippa.

As a coast defence a fortress on this site must have been of great value, commanding as it did the north-western mouth of the Swale, and protecting the water which divides the Isle of Sheppey from the mainland.

Henry VIII recognised the value of this point, and repaired it so as to make it suitable for use as one of his coast castles.

The plan of the mediaeval fortress, as might be expected when one remembers who designed it, is ingenious and remarkable.

FIG. 24. PLAN OF QUEENBOROUGH CASTLE, KENT

FIG. 25. QUEENBOROUGH CASTLE, 1784

The main interest of this castle consists in its plan, which proves it to have been perhaps the earliest example of a fort as distinct from a typical castle of the middle ages, in which there was always a certain amount of accommodation for dwelling-house purposes. Queenborough Castle contained, mainly in its six lofty circular towers, more than fifty rooms, but these were of small size. The building of the castle was commenced in 1361 and finished about the year 1367. The plan was curiously symmetrical, and not unlike that of Camber Castle, built in the time of Henry VIII, but the elevations of the two fortresses display great differences. The lofty towers of Queenborough, serviceable enough in the fourteenth century when artillery attacks offered no serious menace, are wanting in Camber Castle, built in the sixteenth century, and their place is taken by low squat towers which offered little surface for cannon-shot.

Canterbury.—There were really two castles at Canterbury in quite early times. The first, largely perhaps of earthwork, was the work of Duke William of Normandy, and was constructed on and near what is now the most southern point of the city wall. The purpose of the first castle was to dominate and overawe the inhabitants of the city, and also to furnish a convenient post for observing the surrounding country. The castle was provided with a lofty moated mound for this particular purpose. The hill called the Dane John has sometimes been confounded with the original mound of the castle, but as a matter of fact the two were not related in any way, the castle mound having been destroyed many years ago, whilst that known as the Dane John was erected in the eighteenth century.

The masonry castle, the ruined keep of which stands to the northwest of the earlier castle, was built by Henry II between 1166 and 1174. The keep measures in plan 88 feet by 80 feet, and, owing to the upper storey having been pulled down in 1817, measures now only 45 feet in height. The castle was originally enclosed by a rampart and wall with several towers, and had its own gate to the city, and a barbican on its eastern side.

The city of Canterbury was enclosed by a wall built about the same time as the castle (1166-1174). There were seven gates in the wall giving access to the city, *viz.*: (1) Newingate, or St. George's Gate; (2) Ridingate; (3) Worthgate; (4) Westgate; (5) Northgate; (6) Burgate; and (7) Queeningate. From the evidence of various old engravings it is apparent that several of the gates had been rebuilt at different

Fig. 26. Canterbury Castle in the Eighteenth Century

times. Westgate, the only one of the group which now survives, was erected in the reign of Richard II, and is an unusually good example of the mediaeval town-gate furnished, as it once was, with portcullis, machicolations, and other apparatus for defence. It is also a building of great beauty both of masonry and proportion.

Broadstairs.—This small town on the north-east coast of Kent, which in former times did a good deal of trade in connection with the North Sea fishing, still retains considerable traces of a gate, probably of the fifteenth century, which commanded the only means of access from the harbour to the town through a cutting in the chalk cliff. It is known as York Gate, and although altered and repaired, still possesses the massive lower part of the original gateway of flint and stone, and the grooves for the portcullis.

Sandwich.—The chief traces of the fortifications of this ancient and once important town are an earthen rampart or wall of considerable extent, a deep fosse, and two interesting and picturesque gates.

We know that Sandwich once possessed a castle, and this probably in Anglo-Saxon times, but its site is a matter of uncertainty. It must be borne in mind that for many centuries Sandwich was the principal port for traffic and merchandise to and from the Continent. It possessed a mint in the Anglo-Saxon period, doubtless in the castle, and times out of number it has taken an important part in repelling invading enemies and in preserving the peace and liberty of our shores.

The Fisher Gate, although buried to some depth in an accumulation of soil, retains several interesting features. One can still see the grooves for its portcullis and the recessed space in its outer wall into which the drawbridge fitted when drawn up. The gate is constructed of flints and stone, a certain proportion of which are squared blocks of sandstone, which from their size and shape may well have been derived from the walls of the ruined *castrum* of Richborough, less than two miles distant.

The Barbican is a peculiarly picturesque structure commanding the entrance to the town on the south-east side by the ancient ferry across the river Stour, which at this point is tidal and often rapid and deep. There is a modern bridge. The gateway, which is flanked by two towers presenting externally semicircular walls, is largely of Tudor masonry, arranged in chess-board fashion in black flint and grey stone, and long flat bricks. On the southern side of the gateway a modern door has been made into the south tower. Splayed embrasures com-

FIG. 27. THE FISHER GATE, SANDWICH, KENT

FIG. 28. THE BARBICAN GATE, SANDWICH, KENT

manding the approach are visible within the tower. According to local tradition these were intended for cannon. The upper part of the gate is a modern restoration in woodwork.

Sandwich originally possessed five gates, but those described are the only two which have survived.

Dover Castle.—For the last seven and a half centuries Dover Castle has been justly considered a fortress of paramount importance in the defence of England. Its site is remarkable for more than one reason. The steepness of the chalk cliffs towards the sea, and the abruptness of the other slopes, natural and artificial, which encircle it on the land side, give a peculiarly difficult, indeed, impregnable character to the fortress. The height of the hill on which the castle stands close to the narrowest part of the Channel which separates our shores from those of the Continent renders it a spot of unusual importance for the purposes of observing the approach of an enemy coming across the Straits of Dover.

Although there are no certain traces of defensive works on the eastern heights of Dover before the time of the Norman Conquest, the natural advantages of the site, and Caesar's own words make it probable that some kind of camp or look-out post was established at Dover in prehistoric times. However, this is a matter of conjecture which lacks the confirmation of actual archaeological evidence.

One of the first acts of the Norman Conqueror was to establish his power over the English by building earthwork castles, and such a work was thrown up on the eastern heights of Dover. Its form and extent are unknown, but it may, with reasonable probability, be conjectured that its central eminence was that upon which the keep was subsequently erected in the reign of Henry II.

Dover Castle, as it exists today, presents a good example of the amalgamated defences of several different architectural periods. Its important position as the *Clavis et repagulum Angliae*, gives it a national rather than local importance, and every part of it is of historical interest. As a fortress which from Norman times, almost without intermission to the present day, has retained its garrison and maintained a foremost place in the defence of the realm, Dover Castle deserves more than a passing notice in these pages.

During the reign of Henry I (1100-1135) masonry began to take the place of earthwork defences, but in due time the need of stronger defences became apparent, and during the reign of Henry II (1154-

1189) the keep, citadel, and defensive works to the north were carried out at the enormous expense of nearly £5,000.

The keep, one of the most important of the new works, forms a striking feature of the castle. In plan it is practically square, measuring 98 feet by 96 feet, exclusive of the fore-building, with walls at the lowest stage no less than 24 feet in thickness. This is amongst the largest buildings of its class in this country. Each of its three floors, basement, and first and second storeys, is occupied by two large apartments, those on the second floor being the chief or state apartments and possessing two tiers of windows.

Dover Castle suffered a siege in 1137, and again in 1216. The latter occurred under the second constableship of Hubert de Burgh at the hands of the Dauphin Louis of France. (*See Part 5 the section on the Cinque Ports.*)

After this siege Dover Castle was strengthened by the construction of an additional defensive work, commanding the plateau to the north of the castle, and other works, including a subterranean passage, excavated in the solid chalk, which still exists. These works were carried out between 1220 and 1239. In 1371 a series of important repairs was effected, and during the reign of Edward IV the Clopton tower was rebuilt, and a sum of £10,000 was expended in placing Dover Castle in a state of thorough repair.

Further important works were carried out by Henry VIII in connection with his great scheme of coast defence. In addition to the strengthening of the actual works of the castle, it appears that "bulwarks under Dover Castle," probably near the level of the sea-shore, and a "bulwark in the cliff" were constructed at this period. An interesting plan of Dover, made in the time of Queen Elizabeth, shows not only the Arckcliffe Bulwark and the Black Bulwark, but also the walls and its towers inclosing the town of Dover. The plan was published in the sixth volume of *Archaeologia*, and is here reproduced in much reduced size by permission of the Society of Antiquaries.

In June 1666, and again in July 1667, an invasion of Dover by the Dutch fleet was expected. The invasion of this particular part of the sea-coast was never carried out, but the castle was provisioned for a siege, and it is probable that the actual fortifications were improved and augmented.

In the earlier part of the eighteenth century Dover Castle appears to have been much neglected, and an engraved view by Buck, published in or about the year 1735, indicates that certain parts of it had

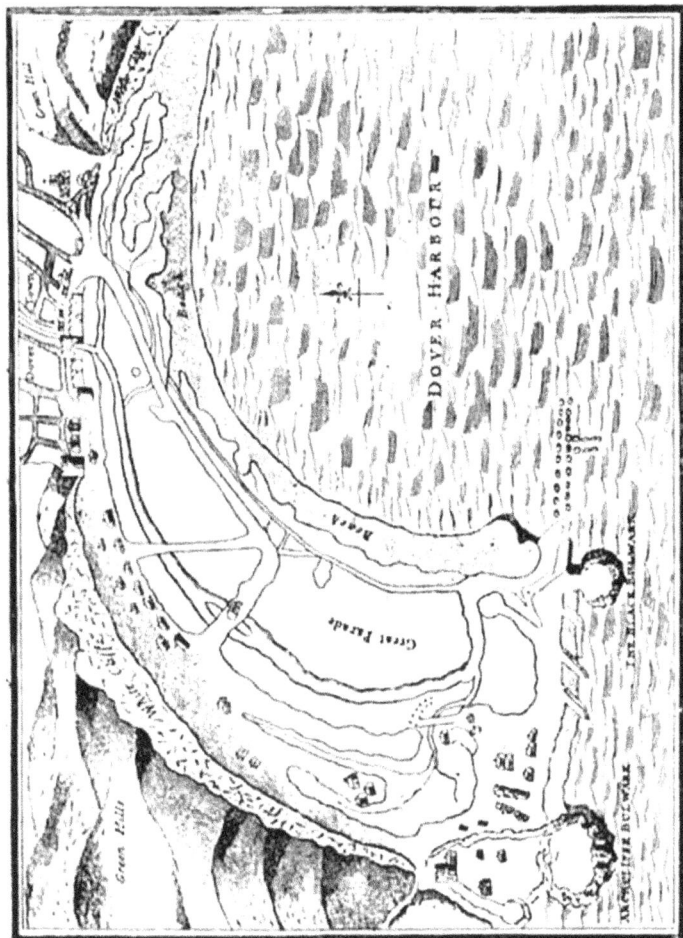

FIG. 29. BIRD'S-EYE VIEW OF DOVER TOWN AND HARBOUR, *TEMP.* QUEEN ELIZABETH

become almost ruinous; but in 1779, owing to the war with our colonies, as well as France and Spain, Dover Castle was hastily placed in a state of extra defence in order to resist the threatened invasion by our enemies.

The period of the Napoleonic menace saw great improvements at Dover Castle. Much of the underground work on the north side of the castle, as well as in other parts, belongs to this period. Of these and later works it is not necessary to speak in this volume. They belong to defences which are still effective, and at the present moment Dover Castle may be regarded as a fortress of enormous importance in the safe-guarding of our shores.

Folkestone.—No traces remain here of defensive work, but a castle was built in quite early times, by William de Arcis, for the protection of the town. Owing to the fall of the cliffs and the inroads of the sea, this has long since been destroyed. It is probable that there was some kind of protective work near the mouth of the little river which here runs into the sea, but no traces seem to remain.

Saltwood.—Situated about two miles inland from Hythe, this castle can hardly be described as a purely coast fortress, but it is such a valuable example of the mediaeval castles of its time that it deserves special attention. It must be remembered that the typical mediaeval castle, with its elaborate defences, possessed a moral influence out of all proportion to its strategic value. As soon as effective charges of gunpowder were employed the weakness of mere walls of masonry became at once apparent. Explosives were far more effective and disconcerting than battering-rams.

Experience extending over many centuries teaches, what has been so thoroughly proved by recent events on the Continent, that offensive tactics are almost invariably preferable to those of a defensive character, even when practised under the protection of the strongest and most elaborate fortifications.

Still, as long as the only dangers were starvation and battering-rams, the mediaeval castle was as nearly as possible a perfect form of defence. Saltwood Castle furnishes an excellent example of this.

Its main structure is of late fourteenth century date. Elaborate and complicated defences guarded the main entrance to the mediaeval castle. Before the unwelcome visitor could enter, the following obstacles had to be surmounted. First was the gateway in the outer wall of defence, access to which was by means of a drawbridge spanning

Fig. 30. The Gate-House, Saltwood Castle, Kent

a deep but perhaps dry moat. This first gateway was furnished with portcullis, and heavy timber doors capable of offering formidable resistance. The outer gateway passed, the invaders would proceed across the outer bailey towards the inner and far stronger gatehouse, exposed all the while to such missiles, arrows, cross-bow bolts, etc., as might be projected from the battlements and loop-holes of the castle.

Here, at the entrance to the great gatehouse, the moat was generally wide, deep, and filled with water. Supposing that the drawbridge was down (a most unlikely circumstance), the enemy on approaching the gates was confronted by the massive portcullis, and at least two pairs of double timber gates beyond it, and whilst forcing the former he would be within the range of heavy stones and every kind of dangerous and unpleasant missile dropped or thrown from the machicolations situated between the flanking towers almost on a level with the battlements above. The massive and studded oak doors were constructed of a material which was not easily fired, and they were barred with oak beams of the strength and almost the consistency of steel. Even when these were burnt or battered down the invaders would encounter a flanking fusillade from the lateral passages.

On the other hand, if the drawbridge was up, it formed in itself an extremely formidable barrier, because by means of chains passing through holes in the wall it was drawn close to the gatehouse tower and within the recess specially made to receive it, leaving the under side of the bridge flush with the surface of the gatehouse wall.

It may be doubted whether anything in the whole range of military architecture furnishes a more perfect system of defence than the gateway, walls, ditches, moats, and drawbridges of a mediaeval castle; and it seems probable that it would have proved invulnerable against a direct attack from without had not the discovery of gunpowder put a new and terrible weapon in the hands of the attacking force.

Elaborate precautions were taken to secure the walls of mediaeval castles from attack. Experience proved that the massive masonry of Norman times was inadequate. A new principle was universally adopted. The plan of the castle was so arranged that every part of the enclosing wall was commanded by means of mural towers. These additions not only added to the passive strength of the work, but also when placed within a bow-shot distance enabled the defenders, themselves protected, to enfilade the intermediate curtain. Again, the use of curved walls and mural towers gave free scope for constructive skill and favoured the economical use of building materials.

Rye.—Wall and gates were built by Edward III. Of these the Land-gate remains. The Ypres Tower, a work of the time of King Stephen, also survives. The first wall was built in the time of Richard I, and of this there are no traces, whilst of the wall built by Edward III one finds very few traces.

Winchelsea.—This town also was formerly walled and defended by strong gates. Of the latter three still survive, *viz.*, Strand Gate, New Gate, and Land Gate.

Hastings.—This was the first castle built in England by the Normans after the Norman Conquest, and, in accordance with the plan of other fortresses of the period, consisted of a mound (shown in the Bayeux tapestry) and two, if not three, attached baileys. One of the baileys, called "Ladies Parlour," is of rather small size, comprising little more than one acre, a circumstance which has led Mr. Harold Sands, F.S.A., an eminent authority on castles, to infer that it could not have been the outer bailey. His inference was confirmed by the discovery of the traces of another, and much larger, bailey, containing about five acres, situated on the eastern and northern sides.

The masonry part of the castle was probably erected in the years 1171 and 1172. Further important parts of the castle were subsequently built, notably in 1173-4, etc. The fall of the sandstone cliff, due to the inroads of the sea, has destroyed a very large part of these works, and what remains is a comparatively small part of the area of the castle.

The castle at Hastings mentioned in the *Anglo-Saxon Chronicle* as having been built by the order of Robert, Earl of Mortain, is not to be confounded with that fortress whose ruins crown the hill overlooking Hastings. It was probably situated on the shore of the western, or Priory valley at a point near the site of the present railway station.

It may not be generally known that in former times Hastings was protected on the sea side by a wall. This wall, which had a gateway and portcullis, extended from the Castle Hill to the East Hill, and was so arranged as to cut off the valley of the Bourne from the shore. A portion of the wall is figured as being in existence in 1824, when *The History and Antiquities of Hastings* was published by W. G. Moss. Slight traces of the wall may still be seen. The steep character of the hills of the Bourne valley rendered walls unnecessary on either side. This wall at Hastings is in some ways comparable with the defensive gate at Broadstairs already described.

A little to the west of this wall, situated on the very edge of the shore, was formerly a fort, the memory of which is preserved in local names.

Pevensey.—The Roman *castrum* here, with its very interesting masonry, has been described in the earlier part of this volume. Reference has also been made to the construction of a mediaeval castle within its area. It has long been supposed that there had been a Norman keep, and this has been confirmed by recent excavation and examination of the site.

Bramber.—An early earthwork, possibly a Danish camp, at Bramber, has already been mentioned. The site was granted by William the Conqueror to William de Broase, and a massive castle, of which certain ruins remain, was erected by him. It is now, owing to modifications of our river systems, somewhat remote from the main stream of the Shoreham River (incorrectly called the Adur), but there is every reason to believe that at the time of the Danes, and probably long after, it had a direct communication by water with the sea. Shoreham itself, it may be added, in 1346, furnished no less than twenty-six ships for Edward III's invasion of France.

Portsmouth.—The existence of remains of the Roman *castrum* at Porchester, situated on the upper waters of Portsmouth Harbour, goes to show that in those early times the value of this part of the coast as a great harbour was recognized. It is curious, therefore, that no town of any importance was built at Portsmouth until the twelfth century. The actual building of the town was commenced in the reign of Richard I, and a charter was granted in the year 1194. Confirmation of this charter was made at various dates by successive sovereigns, and important additions to the privileges were made in 1627 by Charles I.

The town itself was defended by a wall with towers and gates, the date of which is not clear; but from the position of the place on the south coast, and open in a peculiar degree to invasion by the French, it is reasonable to infer that the defences were made at an early period in the history of the town, probably in the thirteenth or fourteenth centuries.

Leland in his *Itinerary* describes the defences as consisting of a "mudde waulle armid with tymbre, whereon be great peaces both of yron and brassen ordinaunces." The circuit of the town was a mile, and a ditch was constructed outside the wall. Leland records that he heard in the town that the defences of the entrance to the harbour

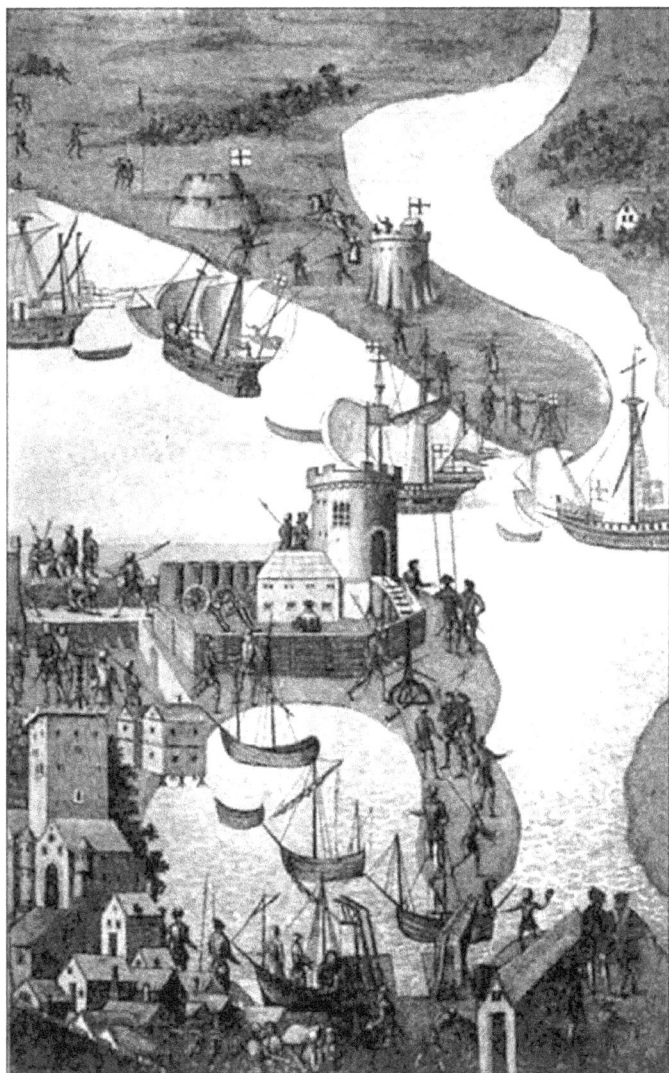

FIG. 31. Entrance to Portsmouth Harbour, *temp.*
King Henry VIII

FIG. 32. SOUTHSEA CASTLE, *TEMP.* KING HENRY VIII

("the tourres in the hauen mouth") were commenced in the reign of
Edward IV, continued in the time of Richard II, and finished in that
of Henry VII. In the time of Edward VI two towers of stone were
built, one on either side, at the mouth of Portsmouth Harbour, and a
chain of immense weight and strength was placed between them in
such a way as to form a defence against the advance of the ships of the
enemy. The actual chain, with large long links, is shown on a plan of
Portsmouth of the time of Queen Elizabeth. [6]

The approaches to Portsmouth, east and west, were commanded
by several forts and the two blockhouses, popularly known as Southsea Castle and Hurst Castle, both works being of the time of Henry
VIII.

An extremely interesting picture, in the nature of a bird's-eye view,
of the defences of Portsmouth and the adjacent coast-line, extending as far as the northern shores of the Isle of Wight, is given in the
engraving showing the encampment of the English forces near Portsmouth, 1545, published many years ago by the Society of Antiquaries
of London. The original of this picture perished in the fire which destroyed Cowdray House, the mansion of Viscount Montague, at Mid-
hurst, Sussex, but fortunately the Society of Antiquaries has preserved
for us the copy of a picture which is full of interest, as illustrating the
mediaeval walls of Portsmouth and the castles, forts, and other works
as well as the guns, ammunition, and methods of working them, in
vogue for the defence of the coast about the middle of the sixteenth
century. One can see, too, the two towers built at the mouth of the
harbour for carrying the chain which once protected it. The picture
also comprises a bird's-eye view of the naval forces of England and
France drawn up in battle order at the commencement of the action
between the two navies on 19 July 1545.

Southampton.—For many years Southampton took such a prominent part as a seaport, and was such a favourite town for landing and
embarking during the Middle Ages, that it would indeed be remarkable if it had been left undefended. As a matter of fact its mediaeval
walls and towers and gates were peculiarly strong. The walls varied
from 25 feet to 30 feet in height, nearly 2,000 yards in length, and
was strengthened by 29 towers. There were seven principal gates, and
four of them, as well as large portions of the walls, remain. The gates
which remain are (1) the North, or Bar-gate; (2) God's House, or

6. *Victoria History, Hampshire,* iii (plate *op.*).

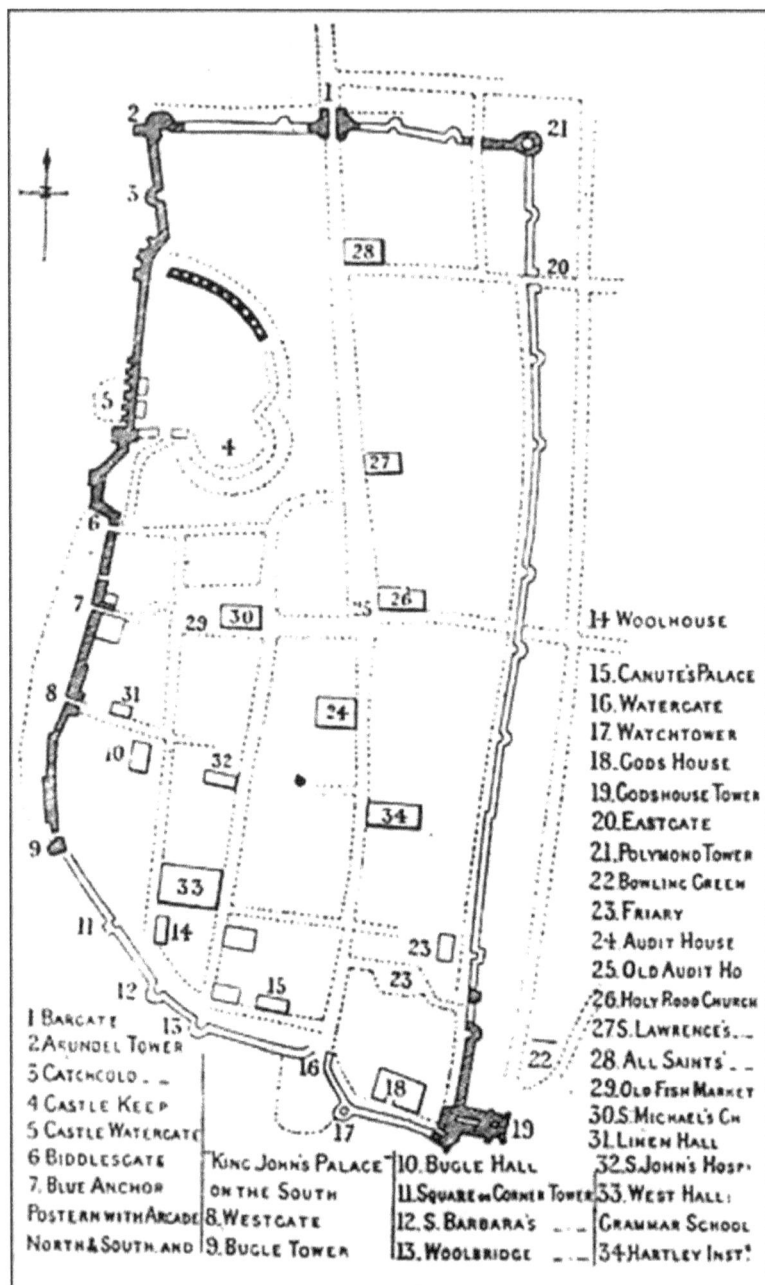

Key to numbered locations:

1. Barcate
2. Arundel Tower
3. Catchcold
4. Castle Keep
5. Castle Watergate
6. Biddlesgate
7. Blue Anchor Postern with Arcade North & South and
8. Westgate
9. Bugle Tower

King John's Palace on the South
10. Bugle Hall
11. Square or Corner Tower
12. S. Barbara's
13. Woolbridge

14. Woolhouse
15. Canute's Palace
16. Watergate
17. Watchtower
18. Gods House
19. Godshouse Tower
20. Eastgate
21. Polymond Tower
22. Bowling Green
23. Friary
24. Audit House
25. Old Audit Ho
26. Holy Rood Church
27. S. Lawrence's
28. All Saints'
29. Old Fish Market
30. S. Michael's Ch
31. Linen Hall
32. S. John's Hosp
33. West Hall
    Grammar School
34. Hartley Inst

Fig. 33. Ground Plan of Southampton

South Castle-gate; (3) Westgate, and (4) the Postern, now known as Blue Anchor-gate. The following have been destroyed: (1) East-gate; (2) Biddle's-gate; and (3) the South, or Water-gate. There were also formerly a Castle Water-gate (now walled up) and a Postern near the Friary and God's House: the site of the latter is lost. The mural towers were chiefly drums, or of half-round form. The masonry of the wall, to a large extent, is of Norman work, and in some parts the walls are rampired, or backed with earth to the summit.

The castle at Southampton occupied not only nearly the whole of the north-western corner of the area within the town-walls, but also the highest ground. Although some authorities have regarded it as a Saxon or Danish castle, the weight of evidence seems to be very much in favour of the view that it was built very soon after the Norman Conquest. It also seems probable that in the first instance it was mainly composed of an artificially-heightened mound and other earthworks, crowned, perhaps, by palisades. In due course, perhaps in the time of Henry I, a shell-keep of masonry was built on the mound, and its wall-footings were carried on massive piers of masonry, 8 feet square, and sunk 15 feet into the earth so as to have the benefit of the original hard surface. The other parts of the castle were built in masonry at about the same time or perhaps within the next fifty years.

Southampton suffered much from repeated ravages of the Danes, and from various other enemies at different times in the Middle Ages.

Wareham.—The early earthwork defences of this ancient town still exist on the east, north, and west sides. They consist of a rampart of some size with ditch on the outside and another ditch of smaller dimensions on the inside. In plan, the earthworks take a roughly quadrangular form, except that there is no earthwork along the south front facing the River Frome. A Norman castle, of which the mound still remains, was formerly part of the protection of Wareham. It stood within the south-western corner of the town.

Bristol.—Bristol has been a considerable seaport from quite early times, having been engaged in trading from about the year 1000. The defences also date from an early period, as might be imagined where great wealth and interests were at stake. The date of the first castle is unknown, but it is said to have been rebuilt in the reign of King Stephen, and in it he himself was imprisoned for nine years. It seems probable that the earlier castle was one of the regular Norman defences mainly of earthwork, whilst that subsequently built was a masonry castle erected to take the place of or to strengthen the earthworks. The keep was square and built very strong and massive.

The castle was situated on the eastern side of the town, and on ground rising considerably above the level of the river. The town-wall, commencing near the west corner of the castle, partially enclosed the town, following the main course of the River Frome, and then taking an almost right-angle turn to the north-east as far as the bank of the River Avon.

Of the numerous castles and walled towns of Wales it is not, perhaps, necessary to speak in these pages, because it is obvious that their function was not so much to defend the coast against foreign invaders as to establish the power of the English, and to assist in the complete conquest of Wales.

Lancaster.—An interesting and important Norman castle [7] was built partly without and partly within the southern angle of the Roman *castrum* which was built here long before. The keep is of fairly early Norman workmanship. The whole work is perhaps somewhat remote from the coast—a little over four miles, in fact—but being situated on the River Lune, it may well have taken its share in coast defence.

Liverpool.—The castle here is believed to have been built in the year 1089 by Roger de Poictiers. During the Civil Wars in the time of Charles I it was dismantled, and its ruined walls were finally pulled down about the year 1725. One or two forts for the protection of Liverpool have been subsequently built on the north shore, but they have been demolished to make way for new buildings connected with the gigantic shipping trade done here.

Carlisle.—The defences of Carlisle are said to date from Roman times. The present castle is well situated on the highest point of ground within the city, about 60 feet above the river. Its walls enclose a roughly triangular space of an extent of about three acres. The keep, rectangular in plan, measures 66 feet by 60 feet and is at present 68 feet in height. It rose to a greater height originally. As one would infer from the dimensions of the keep, it is of Norman workmanship, but it has received a good many strengthening additions in comparatively recent times. The keep is situated in the inner ward which occupies

---

7. A good account of the castle, with plans, will be found in *Transactions of the Historic Society of Lancashire and Cheshire* (4th series), xii, from the pen of Mr. Edward W. Cox.

the eastern end of the castle enclosure. It is approached by means of two gatehouses, one near the middle of the southern wall, leading into the outer ward, and the other about the middle of the wall which separates the outer and inner ward. The south wall of the castle is of Norman date: the other walls are of both Norman and Edwardian construction. The castle (doubtless as a fortress comprising mostly earthworks and palisading), is attributed to William II. The work was doubtless continued (probably in masonry), by Henry I, and completed in 1135 by David, King of Scotland, who also heightened the city walls.

Carlisle was, perhaps, only in a very minor sense of any importance as one of the coast defences of England. Its castle, its walls, and other defences were doubtless intended, primarily, to keep the Scottish border raiders in check, and to serve as a military base against Scotland.

The general principle of defending the coast by means of strong castles erected near the shore was in due course extended in accordance with local requirements. Thus, Tynemouth Priory, situated on the coast of Northumberland, was provided as we have seen, with a gatehouse closely resembling in form and massive strength the gatehouse of a mediaeval castle. It is certain that its builders contemplated and provided for military defence.

Houses of great personages, and of wealthy institutions such as monastic houses were also built on a defensive or semi-defensive scale.

PART 4

Coast Defences Under Henry VIII and Later

DEFENCES ON THE EAST COASTS OF KENT AND SUSSEX

During the reign of Henry VIII an interesting group of castles, or more properly blockhouses, intended entirely for coast defence, was erected on the coasts of Kent and Sussex. The particular circumstances which gave occasion for these defensive works at this period are quaintly set forth by William Lambard in his *Perambulation of Kent.*[1]

King Henrie the eight, have shaken of the intollerable yoke of the Popish tyrannie, and espying that the emperour was offended, for the divorce of Queen Katherine his wife, and that the Frenche king had coupled the dolphine his sonne to the Popes niece, and married his daughter to the King of Scots, so that he might more justly suspect them all, then safely trust anyone: determined by the aide of God to stand upon his owne gardes and defence, and therefore with all speede, and without sparing any cost, he builded castles, platfourmes, and blocke-houses in all needful places of the realme: And amongst other, fearing least the ease, and advantage of descending on land at this part, should give occasion and hardinesse to the enemies to invade him, he erected (neare together) three fortifications, which might at all times keepe and beate the landing place, that is to say, Sandowne, Dele, and Wamere.

It appears that on Easter-day 1539 three strange ships appeared in the Downs, and as their origin and purpose were alike unknown and suspicious, all the able men of Kent rose, and mustered in armour without delay. Invasion of the kingdom was feared at any moment,

---

1. 1576 edition.

and steps were at once taken to put all the havens and possible landing-places in a state of defence.

As Lambard mentions, the most prominent of these blockhouses, as being more immediately opposite the enemy's coast, were Sandown (now demolished), Deal, and Walmer. The two latter, whilst retaining many of the original features, have been considerably modified by alterations and modern additions.

On a coast such as this, extending from Pegwell Bay to Kingsdown, and directly facing the nearest shores of the Continent, it would be remarkable if no traces were found of defensive works raised to oppose the incursions of the enemy. The need of such defences for the protection of the coast must have been apparent during a considerable part of the Middle Ages, and means were doubtless taken to meet it.

Before the building of the three castles in the reign of Henry VIII, which are about to be described, an interesting chain of earthworks of a defensive character was thrown up along the coast. The most important were the Great, or Black Bulwark, and the Little, or White Bulwark, both in the parish of Walmer. There were also two other earthwork forts situated between the castles of Deal and Sandown. In addition to these there was a similar fort on the site of each of the three blockhouses or castles built on this coast.

There must have been many raids by the French and others at various mediaeval periods, and it can hardly be doubted that these forts took some part in resisting them. Against such an incursion as that feeble attempt by Perkin Warbeck in 1495, when the men of Kent in this part of the county, and particularly those from Sandwich, beat back the intruders, such earthworks as these must have been a valuable means of defence.

Among the State Papers preserved in the Record Office are several which give interesting information generally as to the defences set up by Henry VIII in 1540.

From them we gather that the following castles and blockhouses were at that time newly built in the Downs (i.e., Sandown, Deal, and Walmer) and at the following places: Dover(?), Folston (Folkestone), Rye, Calshotispoynt (Calshot), the Cowe (Cowes) under the Wight, two bulwarks above Gravesend, and bulwarks at Higham, Tilbury, and over against Gravesend, at Plymouth, Dartmouth, Falmouth, Fowey, Torre Bay, Portland, etc.

Christopher Morres, Master of the Ordnance in 1540, drew up a book of "rates for captains, constables, deputies, soldiers, porters, and

Fig. 34. Deal Castle, from the south

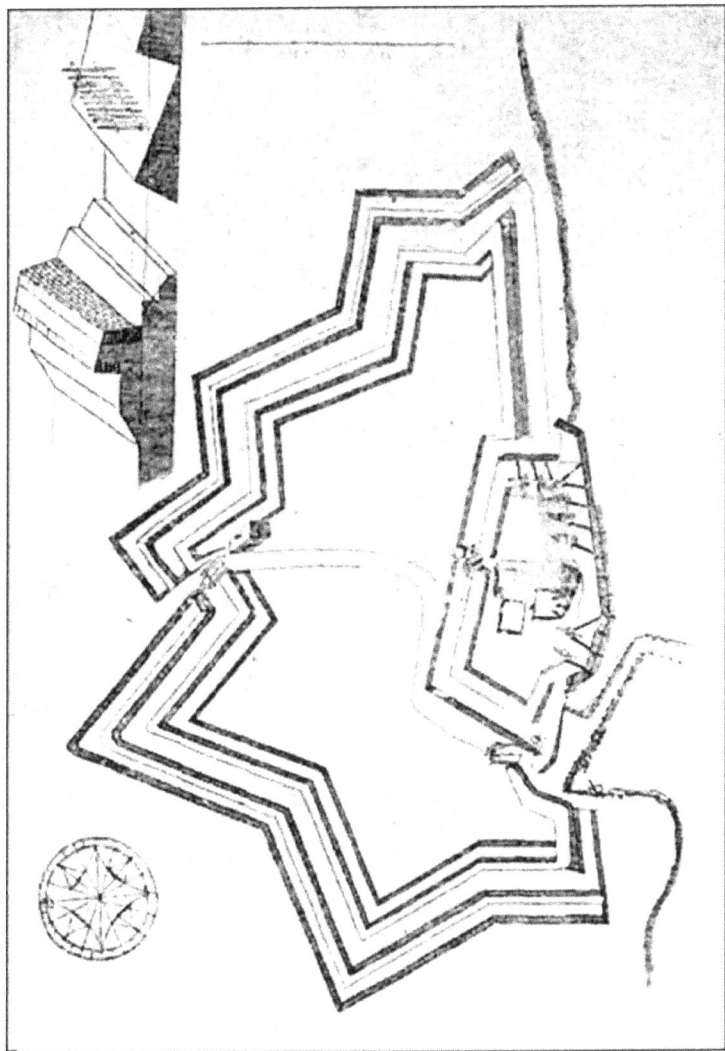

FIG. 35. TILBURY FORT IN THE YEAR 1588

gunners, for the safe-keeping of the King's castles and bulwarks, of late new devised by his Majesty's commandment," in which are the following details:

> The bulwark at Gravesend. Crane, captain 12d. a day; deputy 8d.; porter 6d.; 2 soldiers and 6 gunners 6d. Mr. Cobham's bulwark, Mr. Cobham, captain, and 11 others. Th'ermitaige, [2] Johne's bulwark in Essex side over against Gravesend. Francis Grant, captain, and 8 others. The bulwarks at Tilbury. Boyfield, captain, and 8 others. The bulwark of Hiegham, Jarley, one of the Guard, captain.
> At the Downes. The Great Castle, Thos. Wynkfelde, of Sandewyke, captain, and 34 others. Four bulwarks of earth in the Downs, 4 captains and 32 others. The bulwarks under Dover Castle, a captain and 3 others. The bulwark in the Cliff, a captain and 2 others. The bulwark of earth upon the hill beyond the pier at Dover, Edmond Moody, captain, and 11 others. The Castle at Folston, Kayse, captain, and 18 others. The Castle at Rye, Ph. Chutt, captain, and 24 others. The town of Portsmouth John Chaterton, captain, and 7 others. The Wyndemyll and Mr. Chaterton's bulwarks. One gunner to each. The Tower of Portsmouth John Rydley, captain, and 4 others. The bulwark of Mr. Sperte's making at Gosport side, and the blockhouse there, Slymbye, captain, and 5 others. The Castle at Calste Point, William Shirlande, and 20 others. Total 220 men; £2208. 5s. per annum.

Besides the above, each head house is to have a trumpeter or drum, and the Great Castle both. Crane's bulwark, Th'ermitaige bulwark, the bulwark at Heigham, and the Castle and three bulwarks at Dover are furnished with ordnance and artillery. To know the King's pleasure whether the garrison at Dover Castle shall be augmented or no.

In the year 1540 an act of Parliament (32 Hen. VIII, cap. 48), entitled, "The Castell of Dover," was passed in which reference is made to the fact that:

> The king by his exceeding greate costis and charges hath lately buylded and made nye unto the sees divers castellis blockhouses bullwarkes and other houses and places of greate defence, within the lymittes of the fyve portis and their membres or betwene the same, in the shires of Kent and Sussex for the saufegard and

---

2. The Hermitage bulwark, near Tilbury, Essex.

FIG. 36. TILBURY FORT, 1808

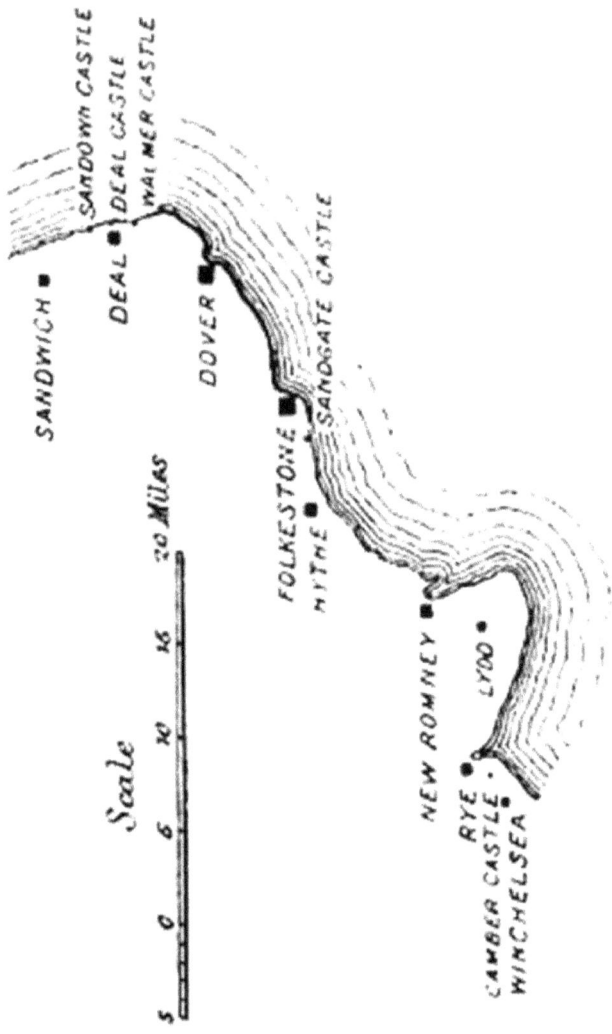

Fig. 37. General Plan of Henry VIII's Blockhouses on Kent and Sussex Coasts

suerty of this his realme and subjectis of the same. . . .

The act is really framed to give power and authority to the Warden of the Cinque Ports and the Constable of Dover Castle, "which now is and comunely heretofore hath ben one personne" over the newly built blockhouses. The act was passed in the year when the building of the castles was completed.

In making a careful examination of these buildings one is struck with the fact that we find a certain unity of idea running through the designs and plans. Deal, the largest and most complicated of the series on the east coast of Kent, has a central circular tower with a diameter of 58 feet, and from it project six small inner lunettes and six much larger outer lunettes. The walls are no less than 20 feet thick at the foundations, and about 11 feet thick at the summit. The whole building is surrounded by a moat and was originally approached by a drawbridge. The circular central tower and the surrounding lunettes, or bastions, are roofed with very thick arched masonry work, and are pierced with 52 port-holes below for scouring the moat, and funnels, or chimneys, were conveniently arranged for carrying away the smoke of the fire-arms. Larger embrasures were provided for cannon. It is believed that these chimney-like openings were intended to be used as machicolations by means of which the invaders could be harassed should they obtain admission to the fortress.

At Walmer, where the plan resembles that of the destroyed block-house of Sandown (the lunettes being four in number), the embrasures for cannon are still left in their original condition, although certain modern buildings have been erected for residential purposes. Both Deal and Walmer retain the chief part of their original encircling moats. This is a feature of some interest as pointing to a new stage of development in the art of defensive architecture. Hitherto, we have seen that the castles which in Norman times presented flat surfaces to the invaders' engines and battering-rams, were superseded by walls having curved surfaces. Curved walls were still built in Tudor times, and for precisely the same reason as those which were constructed in Edwardian days, but the whole structure of the castle was now depressed within a moated enclosure, the aim being to avoid presenting much surface to the enemy's fire, cannon by this time having become destructive and gunners proficient.

Sandown Castle was once the prison of Col. John Hutchinson, the regicide, whose life contains a good deal of information as to the

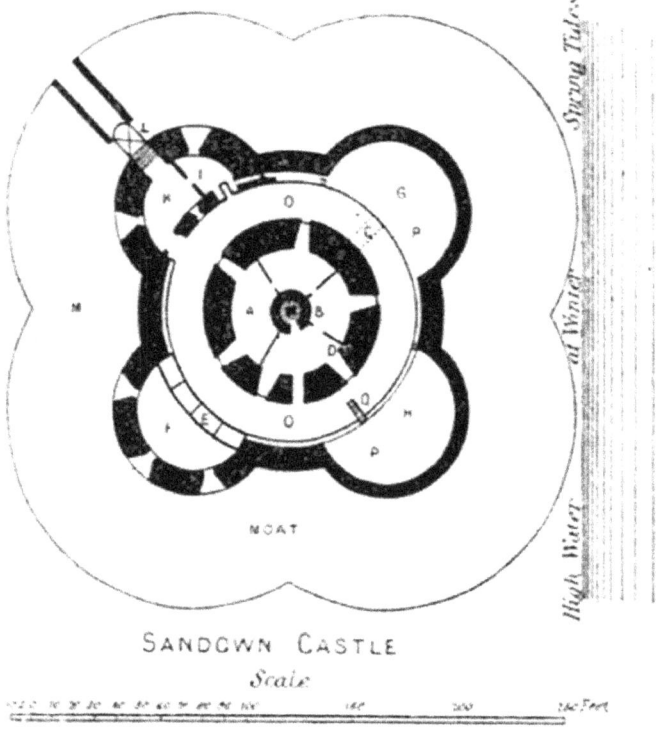

SANDOWN CASTLE

Scale

FIG. 38. SANDOWN CASTLE

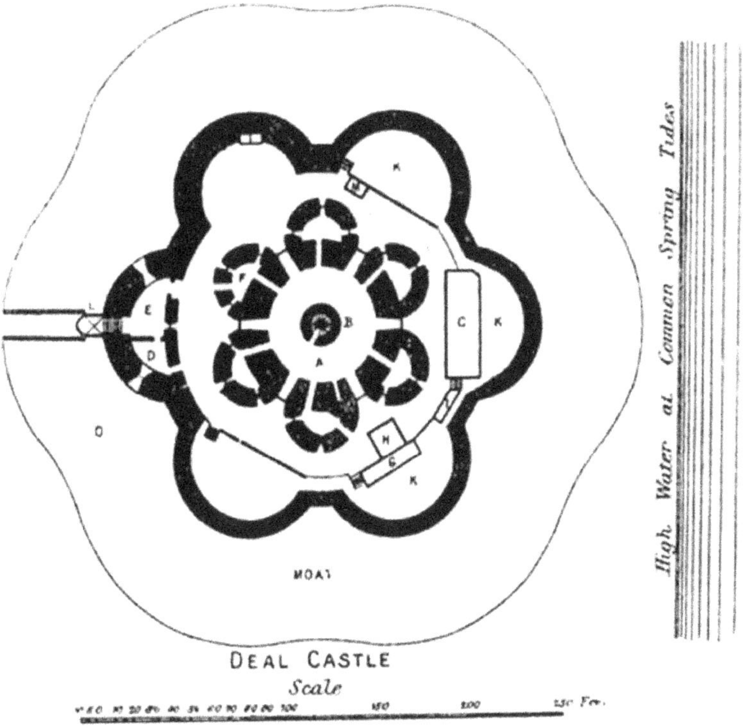
K
C
K
E
D
B
A
F
H
G
K
O
MOAT
High Water at Common Spring Tides
DEAL CASTLE
Scale
150
200
250 Feet

Fig. 39. Deal Castle

dampness and darkness of the place. It stood quite close to the sea-shore about a mile to the north of Deal, and, after being much damaged by the waves, was finally destroyed in 1864. A few indications of its massive strength now survive in a chalky mound.

Sandgate was another of this series of blockhouses, its plan being of somewhat triangular form owing to the disposition of three towers in reference to the central tower. It has been much altered in comparatively recent times (1806), and now stands so close to the sea-shore as to be in great danger of being destroyed in due course by the waves.

Camber.—Beyond the castles opposite the Downs there was one, namely Camber Castle, situated a short distance south-east of Rye, Sussex, which belongs to the same period and was built for the same purpose as the others. Many years ago, however, it had become decayed and useless for coast defence. In 1642 the castle was finally dismantled and abandoned, and the guns were removed. In plan it resembled none of the others of the group, having a central tower and four nearly completely circular towers placed at regular distances around it. Although abandoned for so many years Camber is an excellent example of the kind of blockhouse which was erected by Henry VIII, retaining most of the features unaltered by rebuilding.

DEFENCES OF THE ESTUARIES OF THE THAMES, THE MEDWAY, ETC.

Another group of defences erected at about this period was designed for the defence of the river Thames, the river Medway, and what in later times came to be known as the Port of London. These included blockhouses at Gravesend, Tilbury, Higham, etc.

In 1536 Henry VIII repaired Queenborough Castle and brought its equipment up to date, so as to make it a useful part of the coast defence in this part of England.

Chatham Dockyard was founded by Queen Elizabeth, and for its protection she built Upnor Castle.

Upnor Castle.—This is a rather late form of castle, having been built in 1561 by Queen Elizabeth for the defence of the reach of the river Medway almost opposite the dockyard at Chatham. The engraving of it, here reproduced, shows it to have been a castellated building three stories in height, and furnished with towers at each end. A platform for guns, defended by a stockade, was made in front of the castle close to the edge of the river. The forts at Sheerness and Gillingham were built during the reign of Charles I.

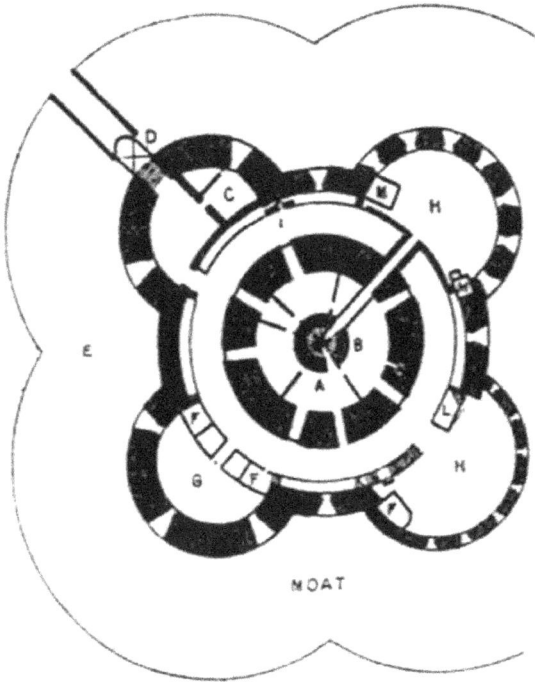

D
C
M
H
I
E
A
B
G
F
H

High Water at Spring Tides

MOAT

Fig. 40. Walmer Castle

Fig. 41. Walmer Castle, from The North

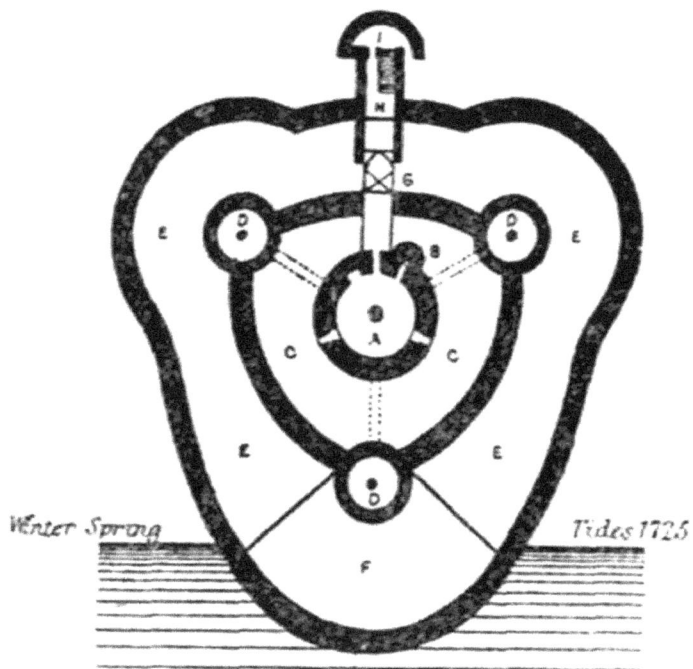

Winter Spring

Tides 1725

FIG. 42. SANDGATE CASTLE

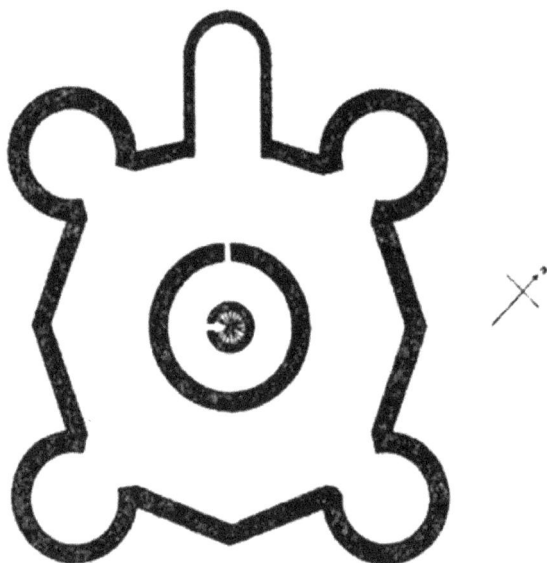

CAMBER CASTLE

Scale,

FIG. 43. CAMBER CASTLE

Landguard Fort, situated on the extreme south-eastern corner of Suffolk, was erected about the beginning of the reign of Charles I, in order to command the mouth of the combined estuaries of the Rivers Orwell and Stour. The first fort having been demolished, new works were built in 1718, and eight small towers, each mounting three guns, were erected on the adjacent coast in 1806. Owing to undermining by the sea some of these towers were destroyed twenty or thirty years after they were built.

Brighton.—In the year 1558, in consequence of the frequent incursions and depredations of the French, the people of Brighton determined to erect fortifications for the defence of the place. A site was selected on the low cliff between Black Lion Street and Ship Street, and about 215 yards westward of East Street. Upon this was erected a circular blockhouse, as it was called, containing in the main storage for arms and ammunition. Beyond it, towards the sea, was a small battery comprising four pieces of large ordnance.

It is somewhat surprising to learn that in addition to these fortifications against enemies, Brighton possessed three gates, *viz.*, (1) the East Gate and Portal at the south end of East Street, (2) the Middle Gate, opposite the end of Middle Street, and (3) the West Gate, opposite the end of West Street.

DEFENCES OF THE SOUTH COAST

Along the south coast, particularly in the neighbourhood of Portsmouth, another group of coast defences specially designed to protect the extremely important naval base of Portsmouth Harbour, was built by Henry VIII. They comprised the blockhouses or castles of Southsea, Hurst, Calshot, and in the Isle of Wight, Cowes, Sandown, and Yarmouth.

Southsea Castle.—Situated about three-quarters of a mile to the south or south-east of Portsmouth, was built by Henry VIII in 1539. The original castle consisted of a blockhouse with a dome-like top. Additions to it in the form of a star-fort were made in the time of Charles I. It was repaired and enlarged on the accession of the House of Hanover.

The castle was situated on the level ground quite near the sea-shore and was apparently selected with a view to commanding the approach of ships from the east in the direction of Portsmouth.

Fort Cumberland.—A more modern defence, having been built in

FIG. 44. UPNOR CASTLE

Fig. 45. Hurst Castle

1746 and enlarged in 1794.

Hurst Castle.—A fortress of considerably larger size than those on the east coast, is situated on the Solent, and was built specially to defend the approach to Southampton Harbour against the French. Its building was commenced in 1541 and finished in 1544. The fortress was of some importance during the Civil War, and served for some days as the prison of Charles I. Towards the end of the seventeenth century it mounted nearly thirty guns. Several alterations have been made to it from time to time. Both Hurst Castle and Cowes Castle were built with materials derived from the fabric of Beaulieu Abbey.

Calshot Castle.—Was a small fort built in the time of Henry VIII with stones taken from the ruins of Beaulieu Abbey. Its special function was to defend Southampton Water. Certain additions were made during the reign of Queen Elizabeth, but the site chosen for the castle was most unsuitable, owing to proximity to the sea-shore.

Cowes (West).—The fortress here, built in 1539, possessed a semicircular battery and mounted eight pieces of heavy ordnance. Its situation was excellently chosen for defensive purposes.

Sandown.—The blockhouse here, erected between 1537 and 1540, was built on a site close by the sea, and received much damage in consequence. It appears to have possessed a landing-stage, as in the year 1618 timber was supplied for mending the pier and planking the platform. Sandown Fort was built on a site a little more remote from the sea in 1631-2.

Yarmouth (Little).—This castle, which was built somewhat later than other members of the group to which it belongs, was finished in 1547. The need for it seems to have been suggested by a raid by the French in the Isle of Wight in 1543. In 1586, and again in 1599, it was strengthened by the addition of earthwork defences.

Weymouth or Sandsfort Castle.—This castle is situated on an eminence to the south of Weymouth, and commands extensive views over Portland Bay or Road. It was erected by Henry VIII in 1539 or 1540.

Portland Castle.—As early as the reign of William Rufus a castle is supposed to have existed here. It has long been known by the name of Bow-and-Arrow Castle, although locally it is sometimes called Rufus's Castle. Its origin and date are not quite clearly known, but it is evidently a work of considerable antiquity, and was probably intended for the defence of the coast.

Henry VIII built a new castle here in 1520, on his return from the interview with Francis I, usually called "the Field of the Cloth of Gold." Its purpose was to protect the coast here in connection with Sandsfort or Sandsfoot Castle.

In 1588 the fortress was garrisoned in expectation of a landing by the Spanish Armada. It figured, too, in the Civil Wars of the time of Charles I.

Holy Island.—Of the two castles on Holy Island, one, known as the Fort of Beblowe, was erected in or soon after the year 1539, and doubtless belongs to the great series of coast defences set up by Henry VIII. The other castle belonged to a subsequent period, and is believed to have been built in 1675.

It is a remarkable fact, that of all the blockhouses built on the coast, or even in the estuaries of rivers, by Henry VIII, built, as we know from documentary evidence, at enormous cost, there is absolutely no record of any of them having been of real value in destroying the enemies' shipping. From some not a single shot was ever fired, except, perhaps, during the Civil War, when King and Parliament were at variance, and also upon the occasions of public rejoicings, such as royal birthdays, proclamations of peace, etc.

It says much for the intimate knowledge of the distribution of our defences that the Dutch, when they invaded our shores in 1667, steered clear of these castles, and made straight for the Medway, rather than for Portsmouth or Dover, or the east coast of Kent, where there were castles of the Henry VIII period, and later, guarding the shores.

One point in the construction of these blockhouses which must arrest the notice of every one who pays any attention to the subject, is the excellent illustrations they afford as to modification of military architecture due to the introduction of gunpowder. This explosive substance which revolutionized military tactics as soon as the art of using it and of making suitable fire-arms had reached perfection, was probably invented or discovered in the thirteenth century. For many years, however, its possibilities were imperfectly understood, and its employment was more dangerous to those who used it than to those against whom it was used.

The castle-building towards the end of the fourteenth century— say the reign of Richard II—was distinctly influenced by the new force employed in attack and sieges. Curves become the fashion instead of flat walls, and by the sixteenth century, when Henry VIII erected this great series of blockhouses, we find that every means was taken to avoid presenting much surface to the action of cannon-shot. The walls were all curved to ensure the shot glancing off, and the whole structure was sunk in a moat, and built in very strong masonry, and with no more height than was necessary.

Martello Towers.—One of the last types of masonry fortifications to be erected, as distinguished from structures which are known as forts and redoubts, was also in idea one of the most ancient. Martello Towers, of which so many were built on the coast of Essex, Kent, and Sussex, were based on the model of a tower on Cape Martello, on the Gulf of San Fiorenzo, in Corsica. They are built of solid masonry, but contain vaulted rooms for the garrisons. They are furnished with a flat platform on top for two or three guns, and access to them is by means of a ladder leading to a side doorway, about twenty feet above the level of the ground. In some cases a deep ditch was cut round the towers.

Many of these coast defences were erected on the south-eastern shores of England as a protection against the expected naval invasion under Napoleon I.

The whole coast in the neighbourhood of Folkestone, Sandgate, and Hythe, and at other points, was defended in this way by Martello Towers, forts, and earthworks, with a view of resisting Napoleon's invasion. At the same period a great military canal was constructed from Hythe, extending inland to Appledore, and then on to Rye in Sussex.

PART 5

Miscellaneous Defences

THE NAVY

The scope of the present volume is to review the defensive works which have been carried out in various ages for the protection of our shores against incursions of enemies: the story of our naval exploits does not primarily come within it.

The first duty of our English navy is, and always has been, offensive, as well as defensive. In times of peace we have been accustomed to regard our navy as our first line of defence, and this is a perfectly accurate description of its functions. But it is obvious that these functions have always been different from, and in most periods independent of, what is generally understood by the term coast defences.

Yet, again and again, the coast fortresses have assisted the operations of our war-ships when resisting the enemy, and to a certain extent the two forces have always been, and possibly always will be closely connected.

Reference to the story of the Roman fleet for the defence of the shore of Britain, and also to the English navy under King Alfred, has already been made, but the beginning of the English navy may be traced to a somewhat later period. It had its origin in the Cinque Ports.

THE CINQUE PORTS

The association of certain towns on the south-east shores of England for the purpose of coast defence is of great antiquity. In the oldest Cinque Ports charter on record, granted in the sixth year of Edward I, reference is made to documents of the time of Edward the Confessor, indicating an origin before the Norman Conquest.

In early times there were, as the name implies, five ports included in this confederation, *viz.*: Hastings, Sandwich, Dover, Romney and

Hythe. Almost immediately after the Norman Conquest, Winchelsea and Rye were added with status equal to the original towns. Thereafter the precise title of the corporation was "the five Cinque Ports and two ancient towns." In addition to these seven head ports, there were eight corporate members, *viz*.: Deal, Faversham, Folkestone, Fordwich, Lydd, Pevensey, Seaford and Tenterden, and no less than twenty-four non-corporate members.

The jurisdiction of the Cinque Ports extended from Reculver on the north coast of Kent to Seaford on the south coast of Sussex. It will be noticed that at least three of the corporate members are situated at some little distance from the sea coast. Faversham, Fordwich, and in a greater degree Tenterden are inland towns, although two are placed on river-courses which afford access to the sea.

As will presently be seen, men as well as ships were contributed by the Cinque Ports for the defence of the realm, and Tenterden received its charter in 1449, in order that it might assist Rye to discharge its obligations. Hence it is that we find a corporate member situated so far from the coast.

The Cinque Ports were established primarily for the defence of the sea-board on the south-east of England, but in the course of time their purpose was extended. In these early times, when England possessed no regular navy, it was the men of the Cinque Ports who guarded our seas. They provided, in return for many privileges they received from the Crown, almost the only form of naval defence which England possessed until the reign of Henry VII. Until that period nearly all the men and ships which guarded our shores from the enemy were furnished by the Cinque Ports, and even after the time of Henry VII they rendered important assistance to the regular navy.

The men of the Cinque Ports seem to have carried on a certain amount of privateering at various times, but there have been times when their skill in seafaring and their undoubted courage have been employed in work of the utmost value in the defence of England. A celebrated occasion occurred in the year 1217, when Hubert de Burgh, having selected the best seamen of the Cinque Ports, set out with about sixteen large ships and twenty small ones to attack the approaching fleet of Louis the Dauphin of France, the numbers of which were no less than eighty large and many smaller vessels. Hubert de Burgh had grasped the important principle of naval strategy that in order to free his country from the danger of invasion, it was above all things necessary to attack and destroy the enemy's force at sea.

Although opposed by such unequal numbers the Englishmen skilfully secured a windward position, bore down upon the enemy as they shaped their course for the English coast, threw quicklime in their eyes, poured into the enemy a volley of arrows from the long bows for which the English were famous, and scattered and destroyed the enemy's ships, so that only about seventeen escaped; fifty-five were captured, and the rest were sunk. The credit of this signal victory in an engagement at sea which may rank as almost the first in English history, certainly the first subsequently to the time of King Alfred, belongs to the men of the Cinque Ports.

The strength of the Cinque Port forces in the fourteenth century may be gathered from the fact that at the Siege of Calais (1347), when the fleet was called out to assist in the blockade and to defend the Channel, the following ships and men were furnished by the Cinque Ports:

	Ships	Men
Hastings	5	96
Sandwich	22	504
Dover	16	336
Romney	4	65
Hythe	6	122
Winchelsea	21	596
Rye	9	156
Seaford	5	80
Faversham	2	25
Margate	15	160

Among the privileges of the Cinque Ports to which reference has been made there are one or two which point unmistakably to an early origin. One is the right of open-air assembling in portmote or parliament at Shepway Cross, and afterwards at Dover, where by-laws were made for the governance of the confederation, the regulation of the Yarmouth fisheries, and to give decisions in all cases of treason, sedition, illegal coining, and concealment of treasure-trove. The ordinary business was transacted in two courts, named respectively the Court of Brotherhood, and the Court of Brotherhood and Guestling. The formal installation of a newly appointed Lord Warden took place at the Breding-Stone at Dover, also in open-air assembly. It is an interesting fact that these moots or open-air assemblies were summoned by the sound of a horn.

The Lord Warden, who is the chief officer of the Cinque Ports, combining therewith the governorship of Dover Castle and maritime jurisdiction as admiral of the ports, may be regarded as representing to some extent the ancient office of Count of the Saxon Shore, although the changes of time and the paramount importance of the Royal Navy in more recent times in the work of defending our shores, have tended to rob the office of much of its former importance. At the present time the actual duties of the post are confined to presiding as chairman of the Dover Harbour Board.

The freemen or "Barons" of the Cinque Ports are often mentioned in connection with this subject, and it may be useful to put on record the following precise account of the subject, written by Mr. Charles Dawson, F.S.A.

A Note on the Titular Rank of the Barons of the Cinque Ports

The freemen of each of the Cinque Ports have from ancient times been termed 'barons,' because they held their lands and privileges as joint Tenants-in-chief of the Crown, by fealty and special Military (Naval) Service. Their title was almost unique, in this sense, that as joint tenants of their baronies they were not like the individual barons of the realm, but barons-corporate.

When summoned to the king's councils, the barons were addressed collectively by writ, a copy of which was forwarded to each Cinque Port.

Simon de Montfort's general summons to Parliament was addressed to 'the earls and barons of the whole of the kingdom and of the Cinque Ports,' and in the year 1293 the barons of the Cinque Ports claimed of King Edward I to be tried for their alleged delinquencies by 'their peers, earls and barons.'

The title of baron did not, of course, apply to every freeman of the Cinque Ports in an individual sense, except so far as individuals represented, by election, the whole of their combarons at each respective Cinque Port.

In the earlier Parliaments the order of nomination ranked the barons of the Cinque Ports above the commoners, and with the barons of the realm, the scale of their fines for non-attendance being identical with that of the bishops and barons of the realm.

There yet remains one ancient custom which identifies the

rank of the barons of the Cinque Ports with the peers of the realm, namely:—that when their representatives perform their services to the sovereign at the coronation, within the Abbey Church of Westminster, they are entitled to assume their head dress at the same moment as do the peers of the realm, and immediately after the Crown has been placed on the sovereign's head.

DEFENSIVE CHAINS, ETC.

The Chain at Chatham.—When, early in the seventeenth century, Chatham had grown to considerable importance as a naval centre, a curious method of defence was devised. A long and stout iron chain was placed across the Medway at the western end of Gillingham Reach, near Upnor Castle, with the idea of effectually stopping the progress of alien ships up the river beyond this point. When the chain was originally placed here is not exactly known, but it was repaired in 1606, and soon after abandoned. In 1623 the chain was superseded by a boom made up of masts, iron, and cordage. A few years later, in 1635, either a new boom or a new chain was placed across Gillingham Reach.

The chain came into great prominence when the Dutch invaded the Thames estuary and the Medway in 1667. It was fixed up at Gillingham either on 27 April or soon afterwards. The published accounts are not quite clear or consistent. The claws for fastening and heaving it up were expected to arrive but apparently were not forthcoming on the date mentioned.

Although there had been a great chain here before it does not appear to have been stretched properly across the river. This was now attended to under the direction of the Duke of Albemarle, who went down to Chatham post-haste to complete the defensive works. The chain, consisting of links made of iron bars, six inches in circumference, was strained probably in such a way that it would not be visible above water, and it was perhaps buoyed at intervals. A small battery of guns was placed on shore at each end of the chain in order to protect it from injury by the Dutch. The *Unity*, a warship, was stationed to the east of the chain, whilst on the west side a Dutch prize was sunk, and several ships were on guard.

The Dutch ships, which had been observed off the English coast 26 April 1667, and off Harwich 8 June, now approached. A letter amongst the State Papers in the Record Office, dated 20 June 1667, tells us that the Dutch fleet was seen off Harwich on the 6 June, but the only result was that a few fishermen were frightened, and that some of the Dutchmen landed and drove off some cattle. On the 10th the navy came within shot of Sheerness, and after some hours took the guns. On the 11th, by degrees, twenty or twenty-two Dutch ships were brought up to the narrow part of the river Medway, where ships had been sunk. Two and a half hours fighting on the following day made the Dutch masters of the chain. One guard ship after another was fired and blown up. The chain was broken by Captain Brackel by order of Van Ghent. Fire-ships were sent to destroy the English ships. The first hung on the chain, but the weight of the second snapped it. The Dutch ships went forward carrying destruction with them. The batteries on the banks of the river and the guns from. Upnor Castle were now brought into action, with the result that the enemy soon retired, leaving two ships stranded.

The exploits of the Dutch in the Thames and the Medway caused considerable alarm in London. Pepys, on hearing of the failure of the chain of Chatham, writes of it as a very serious piece of news, "which," he says, "struck me to the heart."

Another and rather more precise account of the occurrence is as follows: On 12 June the Dutch sent up towards Gillingham a division consisting of four men-of-war, three armed yachts, and two fire-ships. Several of the ships charging at the same time, broke the chain, entered the waters beyond and set fire to the Mathias. The Dutch next dealt with the batteries at either end of the chain, and by means of their guns quickly silenced them. Great damage was done to the shipping in the Medway, many vessels being burnt and destroyed.

It seems probable that at least one purpose of the chain was to hinder the progress of fire-ships which the enemy set in motion against our shipping.

In order to defend the government works nearer London, batteries mounting sixty pieces of ordnance were erected at Woolwich, whilst the defensive works at Gravesend and Dover were strengthened.

About the middle of the following September workmen were employed in clearing away the moorings of the chain at Gillingham Reach.

Chains at Portsmouth, Great Yarmouth, etc.—The chain of Chatham furnishes a curious example of coast defence, wholly ineffective against powerful shipping; but it was not a novelty. Portsmouth Harbour had been at an earlier period provided with a similar form of defence. Edward VI, on the occasion of a visit to Southsea Castle, determined to strengthen Portsmouth against invasion by the enemy. He therefore directed the building of two massive towers at the entrance to the harbour. To these an immense iron chain was fixed in such a way that it could be raised and tightened or lowered at pleasure when the approach of the enemy made this desirable. The fortifications of Portsmouth were strengthened during the reign of Elizabeth (see p. 85).

Great Yarmouth.—In addition to a boom and two timber jetties at the entrance to the haven, Yarmouth possessed a chain for the protection of its shipping.

Hull possessed a chain, and an actual picture of it is preserved in one of the Cotton MSS.

Cowes also was defended by a chain.

Fowey.—For the protection of this town Edward IV erected two towers to carry a chain which was suspended, doubtless under the level of the water, across the haven, or mouth of the River Fowey. Subsequently the people of Fowey incurred the royal disapproval when they attacked the French during a truce, and accordingly Edward IV had the chain removed and sent to Dartmouth. It does not seem quite clear whether this chain, when removed to Dartmouth, was used for the protection of shipping, but there certainly was a chain bridge at this place in which, conceivably, the old chain may have been utilized.

There is reason to think that chains for the protection of important centres of shipping were more common than might be supposed from the few definite particulars of them which have survived. As an effective defence against the approach of the war-ships of an enemy, however, it would perhaps be impossible to find a more feeble type of protection.

Booms.—As we have already observed in dealing with chains, the necessity must have been felt of supporting such very heavy barriers, even under water and by means of buoys. The boom, although introduced quite early, must have been an improvement upon the simple iron chain, because it contained, to some extent, its own means of support. This contrivance, a chain of linked up massive timbers reinforced with iron, and armed with iron spikes was employed, as early as the time of Queen Elizabeth at Great Yarmouth, and subsequently at many other ports. Like the chain it, of course, provided an obstruction to navigation, especially at the mouths of rivers and harbours; but its massive iron spikes, calculated to pierce and damage shipping, gave it a distinct advantage over the chain.

Fire-ships.—These were ships filled with combustibles and explosives sent to drift among the shipping of the enemy. In the action off Gravelines, fire-ships were used with considerable moral effect against the remains of the Spanish Armada, and they materially assisted in breaking up the sea-power of the Spaniards. Seven vessels were charged with combustibles and primed with gunpowder. As they neared the Spanish ships their appearance created panic. The Spaniards, in order to avoid the danger of fire, cut their ships adrift, and serious damage was caused by the collisions which ensued.

In 1667, again, fire-ships were employed in the daring raid made by the Dutch in the Thames and Medway. This time they were used by the Dutch near the chain at Gillingham Reach.

Catamarans.—Another method of firing an enemy's shipping was by means of a kind of raft charged with combustibles. The idea of the Catamaran, as regards both its name and construction, was borrowed from the coasts of India and Ceylon where a raft made of three long timbers lashed together, the middle timber being the longest, is used for fishing purpose. As adapted for destroying shipping the Catamaran may be described as a kind of floating mine. Catamarans were much favoured by Mr. Pitt, and in 1804 they were employed by the English against the French fleet, but they proved unsuccessful.

THE COASTGUARD

The coastguard force is of great antiquity, although it is not known at what period it was instituted. In 1403-4 (5 Henry IV, c. 3) it was enacted by statute

> That the watch to be made upon the sea coast through the realm shall be made by the number of the people, in the places, and in manner and form, as they were wont to be made in times past and that in the same case the Statute of Winchester [3] be observed and kept.

There is every reason to believe that there was a properly organized coastguard force at a much earlier period, although precise infor-

---

3. The Statute of Winchester was passed in 1285.

mation on the subject is not available. Certain manuscripts relating to the defence of the coast of Norfolk, however, indicate the existence of a coastguard in that county as, early as the thirteenth century.[4]

In more recent times the duties of the coastguards included the suppression of smuggling and the aiding of shipwrecked vessels. Another purpose was to serve as a reserve to the navy: but in earlier times the prevention and suppression of smuggling was the main work of the coastguards. Early in the nineteenth century a coast blockade was established on the coasts of Kent and Sussex, and detachments of men and boats were stationed at the Martello Towers on the sea-coast.

It is time, perhaps, to bring these pages on the coast defences of England to a conclusion, and to review very briefly the chief features of the subject. There are one or two points which stand out with peculiar prominence.

Firstly we are struck by the origin, development, deterioration, and final degradation in the methods of coast defence. In the middle and later periods of the Roman occupation of Britain the fortresses for coast defence were built in massive masonry. In the earliest examples reliance was placed alone in mass and weight, and no attempt was made to protect the wall by enfilading. In the works built later on this defect was made good. Protecting bastions gave opportunity of attacking the invaders in flank, and so protecting the wall. In the Norman period, again, and particularly in its earlier part massive keeps of great strength and height were erected for the dual purpose of resisting the enemy by passive force, and of keeping a good look-out over the surrounding country or sea, by means of which movements of the enemy could be discovered.

In the periods which followed, notably from the reign of Henry II to that of Richard II, the art of building castles was constantly being improved and developed. Defensive works were adapted to the new forms and methods of offence.

From that time downward to the first few years of the nineteenth century there is every indication of decadence. The defences became more and more feeble. The "chain," as a serious bar to the progress of unwelcome shipping, reached its most absurd and ridiculous stage during the time of the Dutch invasion of the Medway in 1667, when the "Chain of Chatham" was snapped without the slightest difficulty by the Dutch ships.

As a matter of fact, as we have seen, the coast blockhouses erected

4. Rev. William Hudson, in *Norfolk Archaeology*, xvii.

by Henry VIII have never taken any important part in the defence of our coasts. This is mainly due, not to their inefficiency, but to the absence of opportunity. The same is true of the Martello towers erected along our south-eastern coast when invasion from France, under Napoleon I, was anticipated.

History is full of accounts of attempted invasions of England. Up to the period of the Norman Conquest, well-nigh every attempt to land on our shores was eventually, although not always immediately, successful. But from the Norman Conquest downward England has always been strong enough to protect herself from enemies who have attempted to make a permanent settlement. This is due to the fact that whilst we have not neglected our coast defences, we have not relied on castles, forts, and other forms of land defence. We have maintained a powerful fleet of war vessels as our first line of defence. Experience has made it abundantly clear that coast defence without the aid of a powerful navy would be inadequate to protect our shores. Our navy is, and always must be, the first and most important of our defences, and its special business is not to act as a simple coastguard force, but to seek out the enemy's naval force where-ever it may be, and destroy it.

The Battle of the Channel Tunnel and Dover Castle and Forts

By Thomas Berney

A LETTER

Presented by the author to every member of the Legislature.

Beacon Hall
Norwich
March 11th 1882

Sir,

I beg leave with great respect to address you upon a subject which has long been a source of the greatest anxiety to me, and to which I am most thankful to see that you have given your recent attention in the appointing of a Scientific Committee; and then, I learn, of a committee on the question of the expediency or non-expediency of the proposed Channel Tunnel; "that the Government might give it their immediate and complete attention," and "communicate their opinion to the House before any proceeding" be "taken upon the two private bills before the House."

I have recently read for the first time, in the *Evening Standard* of February 6th, the reported "conversation" upon the subject with Sir Garnet Wolseley: and although the gallant general does not enter into that question, I think I may gather from it, that it would require a permanent force of 20,000 men to guard the approaches on this side of this *tête de pont* of a submarine Railway bridge: the loss of whose services would be a very great hindrance to his Royal Highness Field Marshal the Duke of Cambridge Commanding in Chief, on a certainly simultaneous attack upon our shores, upon one or more points, by a force from Cherbourg.

I saw also the strictures, upon the general's remarks, as quoted from the *Republique Française* in "referring to the hypothesis, that the French might seize on the tunnel before a declaration of war," suggesting that he must take them for "Ashantees." I also saw that some upholder of the Channel Tunnel Scheme asked, as if in answer to the gallant general, "What would Dover Castle and Fort be doing?"

Let me mention, in answer to that theory, that Mr. Charles Alanson Knight, brother of Mr. Knight, M.P., Colonel of the First Worcestershire Volunteer Rifles, was in Rome during all the siege of that fortified city by the French: and that he said, that the embrasures of the walls of it were completely under the command of French riflemen; each of whom was ensconced behind his gabion, with his rifle laid so as to command the particular porthole which he was commanded to watch; and with a string attached to the trigger of it: so that the moment the head of a Garibaldian was seen looking out from it, however cautiously in the early dawn, the string was pulled; and a rifle ball sped its projected course, and probably several others at the same moment, into that porthole: and he further told me, that there was scarcely a single morning on which he did not see the bodies of several soldiers laid out upon the ramparts, who had been so picked off during that morning.

It is, therefore, manifest, that, the wires being in the hands of the French, and the telegraph boy with a pistol held at his head, a body of the enemy, though previously undeclared, could during a night obtain possession of this mouth also of the tunnel; so as to prevent the possibility of its being blown up by the British, or the mine being even charged: while a body of French sappers and riflemen, with their gabions, spades and rifles, could be thrown out; and, before daylight, be in similar command over every embrasure and porthole of Dover Castle and Fort, or of any other various forts that might be made instead of them: and then a column of French regiments, brought ready packed in trains by surprise from the interior of France, would be debouching from the tunnel: so that, before 10,000 British troops could arrive, there would be 20,000 French troops in command of the heights around Dover, and the telegraph at work bringing up 100,000 more on the line, and despatching the inevitable expedition from Cherbourg!

To this a railway or Channel Tunnel Enthusiast may perhaps answer confidently "Oh! The sides of the tunnel will be mined: and there will be underground wires, over which the French could not possibly get command, leading to a magazine!! So that settles the question!!!"

But the simple answer to this enthusiast's theory is, that no magazine or charge could with safety be so placed permanently in a mine within distance of the vibration caused by a passing train; very much less by the shock of one running into a truck of coals. And even if a *loose* charge might bear some vibration, yet even slight vibration oft repeated would gradually consolidate it! And, again, even if the mine were placed at only a quarter of the distance of the extreme range of such vibration, it would be very much too far off to produce the necessary effect; namely, to blow one hole to connect the tunnel with the deep sea, equal to at least the whole section of the tunnel, and incapable of being choked with masses of chalk. Anything very much less would simply provide a current that would carry the French back to Calais; unexpectedly perhaps.

Nor, again, would any passenger, in his senses, go by a train were a charged mine known, or even believed, to be there. The extent of vibration is very great! I have myself, as an undergraduate, been in the Observatory at Cambridge looking through one or other of the telescopes then there: and I have seen the cobweb threads in it vibrate so greatly, from the mere passing of a waggon along the distant road, as to render the Instrument useless for astronomical purposes, till it had passed some way along it. There was then a double turn in the road from Huntingdon; and I suggested that the university ought to carry it straight to Cambridge, to avoid this frequent interruption. It may have been done since. It is also not many months, I think, since a magazine was stated to have exploded; and that the explosion was attributed to some rifleman having fired off his rifle at the wall! A *fortiori* how vast and extensive must be the vibration caused by a passing train; and how effective on a charged mine!

The practical result of such known facts would be, tliat a mine would be made; and that cases of dynamite would be kept at such a distance as to be beyond the effect of vibration, and therefore very considerable, in readiness to be conveyed with anxious care and deposited in the mine; and the galvanic battery ready to be put in action for the wires to be connected in the battery, and the mine fixed, on the first reliable declaration of war with France.

But there again contingencies would arise. The moment that the mine was charged, the running of trains must be altogether discontinued; and a panic among the English in France would inevitably at once ensue: and what British officer would, or should, or could dare, even if he might, to connect the firing wires in the battery, with the assurance, urged in piteous terms, that the Channel Tunnel was filled with English refugees?

In answer to the remark quoted from the *Republique Française*, we learnt from the Pamphlet by His then Royal Highness Le Duc de Joinville; (whether French or "Ashantee," but certainly in command of the French fleet,) that the proper manner for France to declare war with England would be by taking Malta and Gibraltar!! Would those tactics ever be forgotten? Would not the Bazaine of the day add to, or substitute for them as of minor importance, Egypt and the Suez Canal, (toward which France has already advanced as far as Tunis,) the Channel Tunnel, and a simultaneous landing on the south coast; possibly at a point long since decided upon by our ally Napoleon III.?

So that, as already foreseen, the charging of the mine with the dynamite would be prevented; and the embrasures and portholes of Dover Castle and Fort, or of any other forts that might be built instead of them, commanded, as shewn, by French riflemen, engaged in picking off our few artillerymen, commencing with the zealous superior officers! And this more quickly than might by some be supposed! The morning-hour of changing guard would be known. What if a single bullet were sent, at a given signal, into each casemate and battery of both Dover Castle and Fort at that time? Let us picture the scene that might be called

THE BATTLE OF THE CHANNEL TUNNEL AND

DOVER CASTLE AND FORTS.

"A stray shot Sir!"

"A stray shot, sergeant? What next I wonder?"

And where the officer or man, whose head and chest would not instantly be leaning out to see for the smoke, and learn whence it came? Alas! Brave Hearts! The "stray shot" is but the prelude to a volley! Too late, alas, do you learn 'An enemy hath done this!' One alone escapes with knowledge sufficient to commence a telegram to the War Office, just before the castle, thus silenced, is taken by the next regiment of the French column.

War Office. "A telegram from Dover Castle, Sir."

The French have seized the Tunnel. Of the Garrison, I alone —

"Wire cut I suppose!"

And His Royal Highness Field Marshal Commanding in Chief would be distressed by a duty divided between the Channel Tunnel

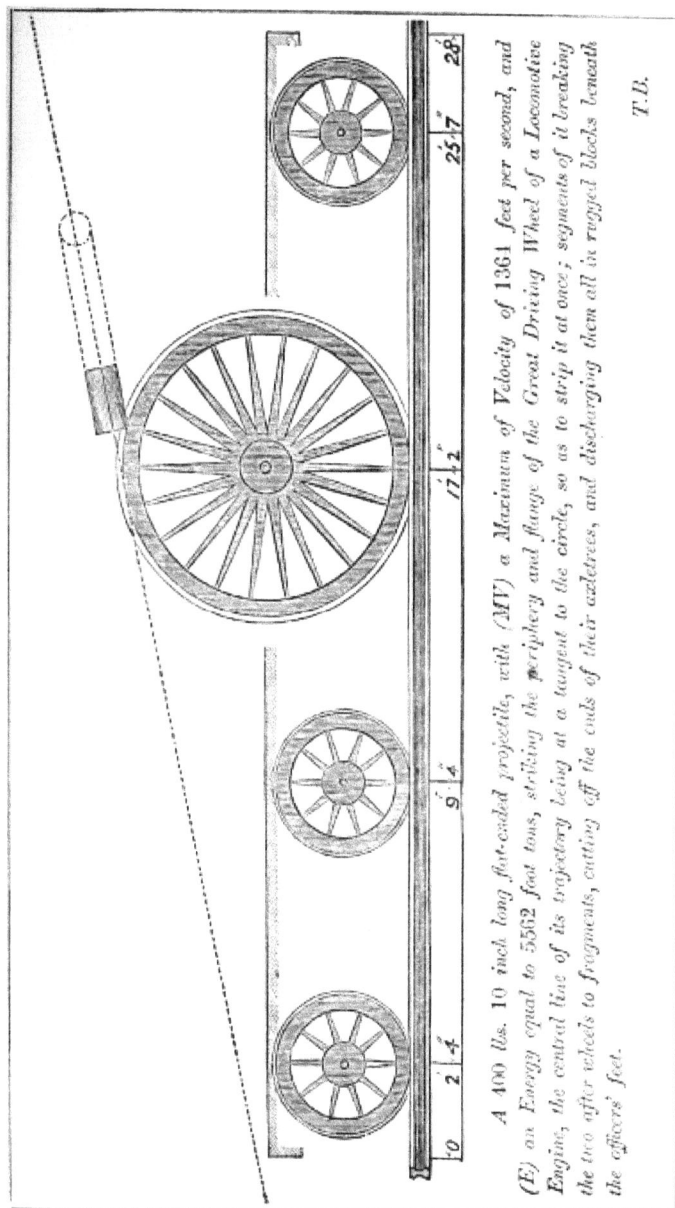

A 400 lbs. 10 inch long flat-ended projectile, with (MV) a Maximum of Velocity of 1364 feet per second, and (E) an Energy equal to 5562 foot tons, striking the periphery and flange of the Great Driving Wheel of a Locomotive Engine, the central line of its trajectory being at a tangent to the circle, so as to strip it at once; segments of it breaking the two after wheels to fragments, cutting off the ends of their axletrees, and discharging them all in ragged blocks beneath the officers' feet.

T.B.

and the south coast indefinitely, uncertain which would prove the greater danger; and with perhaps 35,000 regular troops, nominally, but unluckily on a peace footing, at His Royal Highness' command in Great Britain and Ireland, and perhaps one half of them on duty in Ireland! But what might follow? Let us picture the scene; happily not yet a fact!

Soon a long train, fully packed with a battalion of our noble guards, with the lever of the safety valve held down by the gallant colonel, who has sprung on to the locomotive engine; while his noble young ensign is urging the stoker, and assisting *alere flammam*; is rushing at a but once before heard of reckless speed along one of the two lines of railway to Dover; yet all too slow to keep pace with their high spirits' enterprise!

At length, as it comes suddenly in view, "The castle!" is the cry: and it is taken up from carriage to carriage by the eager guards. They know not yet that it has been taken by the enemy: who have trained two heavy guns to command the two lines of railway leading to Dover; each to the range of a certain spot upon the line lying before it respectively.

Suddenly from one of them there belches forth a cloud of smoke; and it's sullen bomb is heard afar; but not until it's flat-ended long shot, with an energy equal to move 5562 tons in weight a foot, has struck the periphery and flange of the locomotive's great driving wheel near its top, the central line of its trajectory exactly at a tangent to its circle, stripping it off; heavy segments of it smiting the two after wheels, and discharging them in fragments under the officers' feet, and cutting short the axletrees: which, together with the long radial spokes of the great driving wheel thus set free, plunge and imbed themselves in the earth, among sleepers, bent rails and broken spokes and segments, fixing the engine there! Both officers and engineers spring, or are flung, down the sudden decline, to the earth, far away: well is their need! for the tender, bumped by the train of carriages behind, turns up in air; and, making a complete somersault, flies over and beyond it. And the whole train of carriages, with its heavy complement of men and arms, with dire momentum rushing on, piles itself up six carriages deep, (as at the Thorpe accident, near Norwich), in a confused and broken pile, over the steaming boiler; which, like a wild beast in a net, roars horribly!

At a word from the colonel, the noble young ensign, waving the standard frantically, is just in time to save the next train, with another battalion of guards, from rushing with like dire speed *in medias res*. Its gallant colonel leaps from the engine: and the whole battalion, springing out, rush forward to the waving colours, rifle in hand, each eager to be first; and then, as quickly piling arms, rush on to rescue the maimed and the dying, the scalded and the burnt, and to extinguish the rapidly spreading flames.

And many a Victoria Cross is merited for the chivalrous heroism displayed by some of those lying there in their agony, patiently abiding their turn for extrication; like the noble-minded heroine of that Thorpe accident then lying there amid the wreck, with her foot torn off: who, when told by the doctor that he would attend to her soon, but that she had not long to live, is said to have answered, *I will be patient.*—Alas! Is there no Victoria Cross for woman?

And many a Victoria Cross is merited for the heroic reckless courage with which both officers and men risk their lives to extricate and save their suffering comrades: for the French in the castle, possibly not artillerymen, still, having got the exact range, Are at long intervals flat-ended long shot into the living pile: and a battery of eight French six-pounder field guns, having gained the heights, now crowned in the distance with masses of French infantry; and having been pushed forward, and seeing by their bearskin caps that they must be guards who fought at the Alma and at Inkerman, are yet intensifying the horrors of the scene, by opening fire upon them with grape and canister; but fortunately at too long a range. One company of guards, however, seizing their rifles, has sent such a withering hail among them, as they came round to re-load, that many of them bite the earth, never to rise again: and the rest, the limping lot left, are limbering up in hot haste; nor one scathless among them.

And now, having carried all the wounded and disabled, and the dead, out of range of that gun at the castle, and placed them in the second Train, and sent it steaming slowly backwards up the down line of rails; a part saved of the band marching before, and playing the *Dead March in Saul*, to prevent a collision with a special train expected from Kidderminster, with the colonel and regiment of the First Worcestershire Volunteer Rifles, in full Force, for the Front; and the enemy having already shewn themselves in infinitely greater force than was supposed possible; and manifestly now in possession of a submarine railway open to their base of operations, protected alike from British land force and fleet; and of telegraph wires, similarly protected, direct to the French War Office, and thence to Cherbourg; all that the general in command can now do is to fall back with the survivors, as escort; and send an *aide de camp* on the colonel's horse to the nearest Telegraph Office to report all the *statum in quo*; and that the enemy is not only in possession of the Channel Tunnel, but of Dover Castle, and we suppose of the fort also, as it is silent: and that, as for the rest, all that we know is nothing can be known; except that at the other end of that submarine Channel Tunnel railway bridge, now in the hands of the enemy, is France, with an army of four hundred thousand soldiers! 400,000 willing soldiers!!

If these most grave and startling dangers be easy for me, a military man by prescience alone, to anticipate; would. not the completion of the Channel Tunnel cause them, and many more that the gallant general may see, to be constantly floating in the minds of the French, a nation essentially military, till they became like a magazine of dynamite explosive by the smallest spark or jar; or like a mighty, swollen, overflowing river, uncontrollable, and reckless alike of banks and boundaries?

★★★★★★

And now, how will stand the balance of national gain and loss? The Channel Tunnel Scheme panders to the avarice of certain Civil Engineers, who gratify their own vanity, and raise their reputation, by foisting it upon the public as something marvellous; and also a system of ventilation by means of engines worked by compressed air: whereas, First, every Norfolk miner knows, that he can tunnel to any length through chalk: and every bricklayer knows, that if a regular archway be cut through chalk, he can line it with an arch of brickwork and cement to any thickness required.

So far, then, from the scheme being marvellous, an engineering work of which the nation should be proud; the praise is alone due to the geologists who can prove, that the substratum from Albion's Cliffs to Calais is chalk. If such knowledge be assured, the carrying out of the Channel Tunnel Scheme is merely a question of time: and, secondly, *that* comparatively very limited, if the tunnel be driven, as it might be, by the really marvellous tunnelling engine of Captain Herbert Penrice (late an officer in the Royal Engineers and in the Crimean War); which he drives by means of compressed air; which he adopted, in tunnelling through the Alps, with the effect of supplying ventilation in tunnels while he is making them.

Again, the Channel Tunnel Scheme panders to the avarice of the shareholders in it, and in the London Chatham and Dover Railway.

None of the engineers or shareholders may have foreseen the results apprehended from the scheme: but were they to persist in their endeavours to carry it out, after the published opinion of General Sir Garnet Wolseley of the danger to this nation with which it is fraught; and of others by whom his opinion is said to be supported; and, lastly, the arguments herein adduced; they will, I submit, be amenable to the imputation of being most selfish, mercenary and unpatriotic; persons who would sacrifice their country in the future for their own aggrandisement at the present time.

As for the comfort of passengers at sea; suffice it to say, that the proper use of brandy and common salt, if it be applied externally to the top of the head, so as to keep it cool; and a small quantity in hot water, taken internally; will effectually prevent sea-sickness! It has done so with myself repeatedly! and there are little books published upon it as a certain preventive of sea-sickness. So much for *mal de mer!*

And, lastly, as to merchandise; the carriage of it must always be paid for eventually by the Consumer; and justly so!

There is, therefore, no national gain whatever to Great Britain!!!

But, in the other scale. Great Britain has hitherto depended, under Divine Providence, upon the number and excellence of her gallant Sailors; both for safety through the Royal Navy, and for the vastness of her commerce, and for the efficiency of her Mercantile Marine. But every goods and every passenger train, carried by rail through that tunnel, would entail upon this country a loss in the number of British merchant vessels and fast steamers built or employed; a great loss to the shipbuilding trade in each case; and a further loss to this country in the training and profitable employment of British sailors!!

Furthermore, if this Scheme were carried into effect, it would entail upon the nation the permanent expenses of a force of 20,000 troops; and them available for our defence at the mouth of that tunnel alone, or of forts and their garrisons in lieu of them! And, moreover, if through any false alarm, or through necessity, the tunnel were to be blown up, as relied upon by such enthusiasts, the British Nation, through the Government British or French, would have to pay the entire expense and profits lost both of the tunnel and the railways connected with it, English and perhaps French; without ever receiving one sixpenny piece or any advantage from it; whether we remained the British Nation, the Land of Liberty, or became a province of France!!

It is also a rebellious act, in making a breach through that natural bulwark which nature has given us; and which, by the blessing of Divine Providence, has hitherto been the means of our immediate protection, even more than our gallant navy and army: for it was by a storm that the Spanish Armada was destroyed; it was by a gale that the fleet of the First Napoleon was worsted on the coast of Ireland, which he purposed to invade!

Finally, after the opinion of Field Marshal the Duke of Wellington upon the altered phasis of things in respect of the Channel in consequence of the naval use of steam, it will, I trust, be unnecessary to point out, that unless there be the permanent force, as premised, in and about the mouth of and approaches to, a Channel Tunnel as proposed, it would be easy, at an early hour of any dark night, for a sufficient French Force to land near it, and take possession of it, by surprise and at once to telegraph to headquarters for the inevitable expedition from Cherbourg to proceed at once and effect a landing upon our shores!

I will, however, with your permission, state further, in conclusion, that four more recent inventions, than the use of Steam as a motive-power for ships, have very materially affected the relative *status* of great military and naval powers, to the very great advantage of the former. They are railways, telegraphy, torpedoes and dynamite!!!!

1st Railways. The Emperor Napoleon III. considered that he had avenged the loss of 500,000 French Troops, incurred by the First Napoleon's expedition to Russia, by the like loss to the Russian forces in crossing the *Steppes en route* to the Crimea: but a railway brings the military steam-hammer in column, without loss of power, and with its initial velocity maintained, down upon the head of the nail!

In Great Britain we have, at present at least, an insular position. Poets picture "*Our Sea-girt Isle!*" It is Nature's gift. This blessing and advantage, as far at least as still operative, such enthusiasts would sacrifice to their greed by the making of a Channel Tunnel; and would place a constant and inciting temptation in our military neighbour's way!

2ndly Telegraphy. The effective use of this invention for military purposes fully illustrates the adage, "*Knowledge is Power!*" But the telegraph is part and parcel of this Submarine Channel Tunnel Railway Bridge; equally direct to the French War Office; equally protected from British naval interruption: so that, having taken possession of the tunnel, they could at once telegraph to their War Office, and insure simultaneous action from Cherbourg!

3rdly Torpedoes and Dynamite. These are in the hands of friend and foe. Russia is now in possession of numerous long sharp steam launches of extraordinary speed. They are impelled by compound high-pressure and condensing engines and boilers, all of extraordinary excellence of materials and construction; capable of being worked up to 200 pounds pressure upon the square inch; and, at 160 pounds, impelling them at 30 miles an hour!! These launches can be carried on board any man-of-war: and, on an enemy's ship being sighted, one of them can be launched and steam got up with extraordinary celerity: and, on her becoming within sight if the enemy be on the look out, she can, in the space of two minutes, go near enough to launch a torpedo at the ship; and, in two minutes more, have passed her, taking a curvilinear course, and be again out of sight; before the watch would have time to do more than report her presence, much less than to train a gun upon her; and that without the remotest chance of hitting her even in day light: for they are only eight feet in width! And how would the bareness of such possibility be enhanced by the excitement arising from the apprehension, much more from the effect, of the explosion of the torpedo against the ship?

Now these superb engines, boilers and machinery, were built upon the Thames four years ago; and fitted exactly to such a steam launch lying there, the facsimile of numerous launches that were being built upon the Neva, and also by an English firm, for the Russian Government! I have seen every thing and have many particulars. Oh! Defend our Queen, defend our Country from Her friends, and especially from enthusiasts!

Thus has Great Britain nothing to be gained by the making of a Channel Tunnel; but, on the contrary, she has every thing to lose!!!

★★★★★★

May I now, further, most respectfully request, that you will do me the honour of laying this my letter before the Scientific and also the Expediency Committee: as I feel assured, that if brought under their notice by your courtesy, its arguments will receive the earnest consideration they deserve.

And if they, or either of them, wish to call me before them, in respect of what I have here adduced; or in respect of certain sacred prophecies concerning the future, which, if rightly understood by received opinion, prove, that the carrying out of this proposed Channel Tunnel Scheme would be nothing short of suicidal insanity; I will most promptly obey their summons. But, if otherwise, I most earnestly pray, that they will oppose by their joint opinions the passing of the two bills in respect of it now before Parliament.

May I also most respectfully request, that, with the permission of Her Most Excellent Majesty, you will do me the distinguished honour of laying my letter before Her Majesty the Queen; and, further, that you will also do me the honour of laying it before their Royal Highnesses the Prince of Wales, and Field Marshal the Duke of Cambridge, the Commander in Chief.

I have the honour to be,

Sir,

Your obedient and humble servant

Thomas Berney

Rector and sole Officiating Minister of Bracon Ash, in the Diocese of Norwich.

To

The Right Hon. Wm. Ewart Gladstone M.P.

First Lord of the Treasury,

The Official Residence,

Downing Street, London.

LEONAUR

ALSO FROM LEONAUR

AVAILABLE IN SOFTCOVER OR HARDCOVER WITH DUST JACKET

THE ART OF WAR *by Antoine Henri Jomini*—Strategy & Tactics From the Age of Horse & Musket.

THE ART OF WAR *by Sun Tzu and Pierre G. T. Beauregard*—*The Art of War* by Sun Tzu and *Principles and Maxims of the Art of War* by Pierre G.T. Beauregard.

THE MILITARY RELIGIOUS ORDERS OF THE MIDDLE AGES *by F. C. Woodhouse*—The Knights Templar, Hospitaller and Others.

THE BENGAL NATIVE ARMY *by F. G. Cardew*—An Invaluable Reference Resource.

ARTILLERY THROUGH THE AGES—*by Albert Manucy*—A History of the DEvelopment and Use of Cannons, Mortars, Rockets & Projectiles from Earliest Times to the Nineteenth Century.

THE SWORD OF THE CROWN *by Eric W. Sheppard*—A History of the British Army to 1914.

THE 7TH (QUEEN'S OWN) HUSSARS: Volume 3—1818-1914 *by C. R. B. Barrett*—On Campaign During the Canadian Rebellion, the Indian Mutiny, the Sudan, Matabeleland, Mashonaland and the Boer War Volume 3: 1818-1914.

THE CAMPAIGN OF WATERLOO *by Antoine Henri Jomini*—A Political & Military History from the French perspective.

RIFLE & DRILL *by S. Bertram Browne*—The Enfield Rifle Musket, 1853 and the Drill of the British Soldier of the Mid-Victorian Period *A Companion to the New Rifle Musket* and *A Practical Guide to Squad and Setting-up Dtill.*

NAPOLEON'S MEN AND METHODS *by Alexander L. Kielland*—The Rise and Fall of the Emperor and His Men Who Fought by His Side.

THE WOMAN IN BATTLE *by Loreta Janeta Velazquez*—Soldier, Spy and Secret Service Agent for the Confederancy During the American Civil War.

THE BATTLE OF ORISKANY 1777 *by Ellis H. Roberts*—The Conflict for the Mowhawk Valley During the American War of Independenc.

PERSONAL RECOLLECTIONS OF JOAN OF ARC *by Mark Twain.*

CAESAR'S ARMY *by Harry Pratt Judson*—The Evolution, Composition, Tactics, Equipment & Battles of the Roman Army.

FREDERICK THE GREAT & THE SEVEN YEARS' WAR *by F. W. Longman.*

LEONAUR

ALSO FROM LEONAUR

AVAILABLE IN SOFTCOVER OR HARDCOVER WITH DUST JACKET

OFFICERS & GENTLEMEN *by Peter Hawker & William Graham*—Two Accounts of British Officers During the Peninsula War: Officer of Light Dragoons by Peter Hawker & Campaign in Portugal and Spain by William Graham .

THE WALCHEREN EXPEDITION *by Anonymous*—The Experiences of a British Officer of the 81st Regt. During the Campaign in the Low Countries of 1809.

LADIES OF WATERLOO *by Charlotte A. Eaton, Magdalene de Lancey & Juana Smith*—The Experiences of Three Women During the Campaign of 1815: Waterloo Days by Charlotte A. Eaton, A Week at Waterloo by Magdalene de Lancey & Juana's Story by Juana Smith.

JOURNAL OF AN OFFICER IN THE KING'S GERMAN LEGION *by John Frederick Hering*—Recollections of Campaigning During the Napoleonic Wars.

JOURNAL OF AN ARMY SURGEON IN THE PENINSULAR WAR *by Charles Boutflower*—The Recollections of a British Army Medical Man on Campaign During the Napoleonic Wars.

ON CAMPAIGN WITH MOORE AND WELLINGTON *by Anthony Hamilton*—The Experiences of a Soldier of the 43rd Regiment During the Peninsular War.

THE ROAD TO AUSTERLITZ *by R. G. Burton*—Napoleon's Campaign of 1805.

SOLDIERS OF NAPOLEON *by A. J. Doisy De Villargennes & Arthur Chuquet*—The Experiences of the Men of the French First Empire: Under the Eagles by A. J. Doisy De Villargennes & Voices of 1812 by Arthur Chuquet .

INVASION OF FRANCE, 1814 *by F. W. O. Maycock*—The Final Battles of the Napoleonic First Empire.

LEIPZIG—A CONFLICT OF TITANS *by Frederic Shoberl*—A Personal Experience of the 'Battle of the Nations' During the Napoleonic Wars, October 14th-19th, 1813.

SLASHERS *by Charles Cadell*—The Campaigns of the 28th Regiment of Foot During the Napoleonic Wars by a Serving Officer.

BATTLE IMPERIAL *by Charles William Vane*—The Campaigns in Germany & France for the Defeat of Napoleon 1813-1814.

SWIFT & BOLD *by Gibbes Rigaud*—The 60th Rifles During the Peninsula War.